NEW CUTTING EDGE

UPPER INTERMEDIATE

WORKBOOK

jane comyns carr   frances eales

Longman

CONTENTS

MODULE 1

Vocabulary
Types of music

1 Complete the gaps with words from the box on page 8 of the Students' Book.

a **R**ock_____ music is a type of modern music with electric guitars and a strong loud beat. Famous examples include Queen and the Red Hot Chili Peppers.

b **J**_____ is music that was originally played by black Americans in the early twentieth century.

c **E**_____ music is played on instruments using electricity.

d **D**_____ music is made using electronic equipment and has a very fast, strong beat.

e **F**_____ is usually traditional and is often played by ordinary people.

f **D**_____ music is easy to dance to and was popular in the 1970s.

g **P**_____ music is sung by artists such as Kylie Minogue. It's popular with young people and usually has simple tunes and a strong beat.

h **R**_____ music has no singing. The words are spoken in time to music with a steady beat.

i **H**_____ -_____ is a type of music that combines rap and short pieces of sound with musical instruments.

Vocabulary booster
Instruments and musicians

2 Write the names of the instruments and the musician who plays them.

a __drums__ __drummer__
b __saxophone__ __saxophonist__
c _____ _____
d _____ _____
e _____ _____
f _____ _____

Vocabulary
Past and present time phrases

3 **a** Complete the sentences with the time phrases from pages 8 and 9 of the Students' Book.

1 __Back__ __in__ __the__ 1990s, I used to live in Budapest. _____ _____ days, I was working for an international electricity company.

2 _____ _____ late 1980s in Germany, there were tremendous changes. _____ _____ time, I was living in Berlin.

3 _____ the _____ _____ years, I think I've become happier. I used to feel stressed most of the time, but _____ _____ I'm more relaxed.

4 My first passion was cars. _____ one _____ , I really wanted to be a racing driver.

5 Right _____ , I'm studying very hard for my exams.

6 I often hear from my _____ English teacher. He's _____ living in Tokyo.

7 When I was young, I used to hate sports, but _____ I do a lot of running.

8 I love trying out new things, and my _____ hobby is yoga.

b Write seven true sentences about yourself using the ideas and time phrases above.

1 _Back in the 1990s, I lived in Krakow. In those_
days, I was still at school.

2 _____
_____

3 _____
_____

4 _____
_____

5 _____
_____

6 _____
_____

7 _____
_____

8 _____
_____

Revision of verb forms

4 **a** Match the pictures to the sentences.

a _7_ When I feel really stressed, I usually *take* Einstein for a walk.

b ___ If I *won* the lottery, I*'d buy* a new house.

c ___ Jones *was feeling* pleased with himself because he*'d killed* his first bear.

d ___ At the moment I*'m doing* the washing-up.

e ___ I'm looking forward to tonight – I *haven't been* to a disco for a long time.

f ___ I*'ve lost* the cat! *Have you seen* it?

g ___ What a pity! *If only I had* my skates with me!

h ___ When I was young, Dad *used to do* the shopping and Mum did the cooking.

b Using the same verb forms, complete these sentences so that they are true for you.

1 When I feel _____ , I usually _____
_____ .

2 If I won the lottery, I _____
_____ .

3 This time last year/month/week, I was feeling
_____ because I'd/I hadn't _____
_____ .

4 At the moment I'm _____
_____ .

5 I haven't _____
_____ for a long time.

6 I've _____ .
Have you _____?

7 If only I _____ !

8 When I was young, _____
_____ .

Present simple or continuous

5 Write complete sentences, using the correct Present simple or continuous form and making any other necessary changes.

a I / organise / a party for Clare's birthday. Who / you / think / I should invite?

I'm organising a party for Clare's birthday. Who do you think I should invite?

b A: What / you / think / about?

_____

   B: Oh nothing. I / just / wonder / whether to take an umbrella.

_____

_____

c A: What / you / think / *So Solid Crew*?

_____

   B: I've never heard of them.

d What / you / cook? It / smell / wonderful!

_____

_____

e A lot / people / believe / he's very talented but / I / not agree.

_____

_____

f A: Whose bag / be / this?

_____

   B: I'm pretty sure it / belong / Mercedes.

_____

_____

g You / know / Ken? He / be / very interesting. He / work / at the Science Museum.

_____

_____

h I / read / this great book. It / be / about growing up during the 1960s.

_____

_____

Past simple or continuous

6 In this extract from a soap opera script, complete the gaps with the Past simple or continuous form of the verbs in the box.

come	happen	just discuss	just try	not tell
stop	~~talk~~	think		

(*Duncan and Tessa are talking. Carla comes in and Duncan and Tessa immediately stop. They look guilty. Duncan gets up to go.*)

DUNCAN: Hi, Carla. Is that the time? I've got to go. Bye.

CARLA: Bye. (*looks suspiciously at Tessa*) Hi, Tessa. What (a) _were you talking_ about when I (b) _____ in?

TESSA: Oh nothing!

CARLA: Then why (c) _____?
Come on, tell me.

TESSA: Okay ... We (d) _____
_____ Graham's new girlfriend.

CARLA: (*sitting down suddenly*) New girlfriend? When (e) _____ this _____?

TESSA: A few weeks ago.

CARLA: Why (f) _____ me?

TESSA: We (g) _____ you'd be upset. We (h) _____
_____ to spare your feelings.

CARLA: You'd better tell me all about it.

TESSA: Okay. Look, would you like a drink first?

Present perfect or Past simple

7 Tick the correct ending for the sentences.

a I've been to the Pompidou Centre twice
  1 while I was in Paris.
  2 so I don't really want to go there again. ✓

b Denise and Adam have been married for fifteen years
  1 and they were very happy.
  2 and they're very happy.

c I lost my car keys –
  1 I can't find them anywhere.
  2 I couldn't find them anywhere.

d How long have you lived on your own
  1 in this flat?
  2 before you met Lisa?

e Steve's been very depressed
  1 last week.
  2 all week.

f John worked for the company for ten years
  1 and we're sorry that he's leaving.
  2 and we were sorry when he left.

Present perfect or Past perfect

8 Complete the sentences with the correct Present perfect or Past perfect form of *have*.

a Paul failed his driving test because he _hadn't_ practised enough.

b Henry _____ had backache for nearly a year before his wife made him go to the doctor.

c I'm feeling a bit upset because I _____ had some bad news about my brother.

d Carla says she _____ sent the e-mail, but I'm sure she _____ because I've checked three times and it's not there.

e The boys' clothes were filthy – they _____ been playing football in the rain.

f I hope Mrs Reynolds _____ remembered to feed the cat – she's very forgetful.

g I thought I _____ left the report on my desk, but I can't find it anywhere.

h Pierre _____ been working with me for several months, but he still can't remember my surname.

All forms

9 Complete the gaps with the correct form of the verbs in brackets.

Hooliganism

Eighteen-year-old Joseph Willis (a) _appeared_ (appear) in court yesterday, charged with attacking a police car. The incident (b) _____ (happen) outside the ground after the match between Arsenal and Liverpool. Willis, who (c) _____ (come) from Wales and is a passionate Liverpool supporter, (d) _____ (start) a fight with Arsenal fans because his team (e) _____ (lose) the match. 'I (f) _____ (not believe) it,' said his girlfriend. 'Jo's a gentle person and he (g) _____ (never be) in trouble before.'

Jackie Lane: Live Tonight!

'My next guest (h) _____ (never have) any problems with getting what he wanted. When he first came to the United States he (i) _____ (not have) any money and he (j) _____ (work) in a factory during the day and at a nightclub at night to support his family. Now he (k) _____ (become) one of the richest people in the world. Between 1997 and 2004, while he (l) _____ (live) in Florida, he (m) _____ (manage) two hugely successful e-businesses and he (n) _____ (just write) a best-selling book: *Ten Steps to Success.* This week he (o) _____ (visit) his business school in Chicago and tonight he (p) _____ (spend) an evening with us. Ladies and gentlemen, please welcome Simon Bach!'

Improve your writing
Linking phrases for a personal profile

10 **a** Match the beginnings in column A to the endings in column B to make phrases from a profile of a novelist.

A

1 *Born in*
2 *As a*
3 *At the age of*
4 *It was while* she was working in Dundee
5 She had unexpected success with her first novel.
6 *After sending*
7 *As time passed*
8 Now in her fifties, she is *still*
9 *Recently*
10 *Over the next* few *years*

B

a she became very well known.
b she has accepted an invitation to write a television series.
c twenty-one, …
d teenager, …
e as active as ever!
f she plans to spend more time in Los Angeles.
g *This was followed by* a period when she wrote very little.
h her second novel to ten publishers, it was finally accepted.
i *that* she met her future husband.
j Chicago in 1949, …

Writing a profile

b Look back at pages 12–13 of the Students' Book and use these notes about George Clooney, the actor, to write a profile. Decide how you will organise the information and try to use some of the phrases in italics from part a to link your writing.

- appearance: dark eyes and dark hair with some grey
- looks older than he is, but still very handsome
- has had many girlfriends in recent years, including Renée Zellweger
- still enjoys a bachelor life with a group of friends who spend time at his house, playing basketball, drinking beer …
- hopes to develop his film career further
- born in 1961
- grew up in Kentucky. Father was a famous host of a TV talk show
- George loved being part of a famous family – got interested in show business
- twenty-one, drove to Los Angeles – stayed with aunt and did whatever jobs he could get
- worked for thirteen years in terrible TV shows then joined the cast of ER as Doug Ross
- 1984 met Talisa Balsam, fell in love. She broke off the relationship – he had months of unhappiness
- 1989 – got together with Talisa again and married her
- 1992 – he and Talisa got divorced
- major film roles in 'Batman', 'Three Kings' and 'O Brother, Where Art Thou?'

Wordspot
get

11 Look back at page 13 in the Students' Book. Circle the correct form of *get* and complete the gaps with a word from the box.

flight   ~~job~~   message   over
presents   shock   tired   work

a   I'd like *getting / get /(to get)* a better ___job___ with a higher salary.

b   I *got / 'm getting / have got* the early _____ from London to New York yesterday.

c   Sometimes my husband *gets / is getting / was getting* so _____ he can't keep his eyes open.

d   The children never *get / used to get / are getting* many _____ on their birthdays because we couldn't afford much.

e   *Do you get / Did you get / Were you getting* the _____ I left on your answerphone?

f   I *got / was getting / get* to _____ very late this morning, so my boss wasn't pleased.

g   A: How are you?
      B: Much better, thanks. I think I *got / get / 've got* _____ my cold now.

h   I *had got / was getting / got* a _____ when I saw how thin Madeleine was.

Auxiliary verbs
Adding emphasis

12 Match the beginnings in column A to the endings in column B, then add the auxiliary *do* to give more emphasis.

A		B	
a	Come to the party.	1	when people are late for meetings.
b	Ben looks well.	2	but I don't like it raw.
c	I hate it	3	but we enjoyed the tours.
d	We didn't like the hotel,	4	Has he been on holiday?
e	She told us she was going away.	5	I'm sure you'll enjoy it.
f	I like fish generally,	6	Don't you remember?

a   *Do come to the party. I'm sure you'll enjoy it.*

b   _____

c   _____

d   _____

e   _____

f   _____

Sounding interested

13 Respond to each sentence with a short question using an auxiliary verb. Then choose a possible follow-up phrase from the box below.

a   I don't really like jazz.

Don't you?   *Neither do I.*

b   My sister Stefania's got a Yamaha.

c   I'm not going to buy that house after all.

d   Jack's never been to a football match before.

e   I agree with Tim.

f   There wasn't any fresh salmon left in the shop.

I don't.   How long has she had it?   It's okay, I've got some chicken.
Why not?   ~~Neither do I.~~   I hope he enjoys it.

Avoiding repetition

14 Make these conversations more natural by crossing out any unnecessary phrases and adding auxiliary verbs if necessary.

a Do they accept credit cards on the underground?
Well, yes they ~~accept credit cards on the underground~~, but only for amounts over £10.
(do written above "accept")

b The children have been skating before, haven't they?
Well, John has been skating before, but Trevor and Ann haven't been skating before.

c You're not going to leave the company, are you?
Yes, I am going to leave the company, actually.

d Does the flight stop over at Vancouver?
Yes, it stops over at Vancouver for two hours.

e Has the school got a website?
I think it has got a website, but I'll check for you.

f Was it snowing when your plane landed?
No, it wasn't snowing when my plane landed, but it was very cold.

Pronunciation
Weak forms

> LOOK!
>
> The verbs *be*, *do* and *have* often have a weak pronunciation and can be difficult to hear.
>
> • Where **are** you going?   /ə/
>
> • What **does** your husband do?   /dəz/
>
> • **Have** you got any children?   /həv/

15 **a** (T1.1) Listen to ten things that are often said when people first meet, and write them in the spaces below. A contracted form counts as two words, e.g. I've = two words.

1 *I've been looking forward to meeting you* . (8 words)
2 _____ . (7 words)
3 _____ ? (5 words)
4 _____ ? (5 words)
5 _____ ? (4 words)
6 _____ ? (7 words)
7 _____ ? (6 words)
8 _____ ? (6 words)
9 _____ ? (7 words)
10 _____ ? (7 words)

b Listen again and repeat.

Listen and read
A date with disaster?

16 **a** (T1.2) Listen to and/or read the stories opposite and decide who had the worst experience.

b Listen and/or read again and answer these questions by choosing the correct name: Celine, Rodrigo, Robert or Claire.

1 Who had a date by the sea?
  Celine and Rodrigo

2 Who had known the other person for some time before the date?
  _____

3 Who wanted to impress the person they dated?
  _____

4 Who was much older than the person they dated?
  _____

5 Who had an accident?
  _____

6 Who was disgusted by the other person's behaviour?
  _____

7 Whose date was very expensive?
  _____

8 Who went out with the person again?
  _____

c You can use reading to improve your vocabulary by noticing common phrases (instead of single words) in the text. In the following phrases, circle the correct word without looking back at the text, then look back and check.

1 Robert was really proud *for / of* his new Suzuki 250.

2 Claire asked if she could *have / take* a go at riding the bike.

3 She got over-confident and *lost / hadn't* control of the bike.

4 Celine and Rodrigo went *for / to* a romantic walk along the beach.

5 They didn't *have / think* much in common.

6 When Celine saw the body, she got *a / the* shock of her life.

A Date With Disaster?

Have you ever been on a first date with someone you really liked and found that it turned into a disaster before your very eyes?
We interviewed two people who have had just this experience.

CELINE, 27
Hairdresser

The worst first date I've ever had was while I was on holiday in Majorca. I must have been about seventeen, and I met this gorgeous Spanish waiter, Rodrigo. He was a good ten years older than me and had dark brown eyes and black curly hair. Well, after we'd had a few drinks in a local bar, he suggested going for a romantic walk along the beach. Things seemed to be going quite well, even though we didn't have much in common. Then we noticed a group of people standing at the water's edge, staring at something on the beach. We went nearer to see what was happening, and then I got the shock of my life – it was a dead body which had come in with the tide! I turned away immediately, but Rodrigo seemed fascinated by it, and started talking very fast in Spanish to the other people. I found their morbid interest so tasteless that I just walked away … I never dated Rodrigo again, as you can imagine.

ROBERT BUCKLEY, 24
Fitness Instructor

She was someone I knew from school and I'd always really fancied her. I had just got a new motorbike, a Suzuki 250, which I was really proud of. So anyway, one Saturday afternoon, I asked her to come out for a ride, and we went up to a disused airfield a few kilometres away. There was no one else around, so I started driving with one wheel in the air and going really fast. Claire said she loved it and could she have a go at riding it. I couldn't see why not – but how wrong can you be?

Once she'd managed to start it and stay upright, she suddenly got a bit over-confident and zoomed off at top speed towards some trees. As I started running after her, I could see that she was losing control of the bike, and a minute later – bang! She went straight into a tree.

Claire was a bit shocked and bruised, but my beautiful Suzuki was a wreck and cost me a fortune to repair. We did see each other again, but from then on we stuck to public transport.

Real life
Making conversation

17 **a** Complete the conversations with the words in the box.

a	are	better	Could
couldn't	'd	have	'll
's	see	to (x4)	this (x3)

1 A: Katy! What a surprise ^to^ see you here!

   B: Hello, Lev! What you doing here?

2 A: Sorry disturb you. You help me?

   B: Okay, just give me minute.

3 A: Welcome Denmark. I'm Virginia Lake.

   B: Nice meet you.

   A: Did you a good flight?

   B: Great, thanks.

   A: Is your first visit here?

4 A: It's two o'clock. I better get back to work.

   B: Yes, I'd be off, too. It been nice to you again.

5 A: Is that all?

   B: Yes, I let you get on.

6 A: I help overhearing. Are you Portuguese?

   B: I'm Brazilian, actually.

b 🔲 **T1.3** Listen and check.

MODULE 2

Vocabulary
Health quiz

1 How healthy are you, physically and mentally? Complete the gaps in the quiz with words from page 18 of the Students' Book and answer the questions.

---

1 How (1) fit___ **are you?**

a To (2) k_____ fit, I do some (3) g_____ exercise every day, like walking.

b I do (4) s_____ exercise in the gym at least three times a week.

c I start off with good intentions but I get bored.

2 Do you eat well?

a I eat five portions of fruit and vegetables every day and have a healthy diet.

b I follow a (5) l_____ -f_____ diet and take at least three vitamin tablets a day.

c I try to eat well but I snack a lot and I've got a sweet tooth.

3 How psychologically balanced are you?

a I'm generally content and I've never had any (6) m_____ health problems.

b I never show any emotions; I have a great deal of self-control.

c I sometimes suffer from (7) d_____ and low (8) s_____ -e_____. I also get (9) a_____ and want to argue with people, especially when I'm driving.

Mostly as:
You have nothing to worry about. If you continue this lifestyle, it should help to (10) p_____ you from major diseases. Keep it up!

Mostly bs:
You don't like to feel (11) o _____ o _____ c_____ . Maybe you should relax more.

Mostly cs:
You need to improve your lifestyle. If you had a healthier diet and did some exercise, you could increase your (12) i_____ to colds and flu and (13) r_____ the (14) r_____ of (15) h_____ blood (16) p_____ and heart disease.

Forming nouns

2 Read the definitions from the *Longman Dictionary of Contemporary English* and write the correct nouns.

a **m** _usician_____ *n* [C] a person who plays a musical instrument for a job: *a talented young ...*

b **t**_____ *n* [C] someone who is being trained for a job: *The new ... will start next week.*

c **c**_____ *n* [C] the period of time when you are a child: *I had a happy ... .*

d **e**_____ *n* [U] facts, objects or signs that make you believe that something exists or is true: *There is no ... of life on other planets.*

e **g**_____ *n* [C] a person who plays a guitar

f **b**_____ **o**_____ *n* [C] a small tool used for removing the metal lids from bottles

g **a**_____ *n* [U] the cost of entrance to a concert, sports event, etc. : *... is free for children.*

h **C**_____ *n* [U] a political system which has no different social classes and in which the government controls the production of all food and goods: *Do you believe in ... ?*

i **c**_____ *n* [C] all the people who live in the same area, town, etc. : *an arts centre built to serve the whole ... .*

j **e**_____ *n* [C] the pleasure that you get from something: *Acting has brought me enormous ... .*

k **n**_____ *n* [U] being worried or frightened about something that may happen so that you cannot relax: *Minelli's ... showed in her voice.*

l **v**_____ *n* [C] Someone who eats only fruit, vegetables, eggs, etc. and does not eat meat or fish.

Gerunds

3 **a** Complete this article about executive stress with the positive or negative gerund form of the verbs in the box.

| drink (x 2)   get   eat (x 2)   go ~~(x 2)~~ (x 1)   talk   take (x 2) |

These days, being a top executive can be disastrous for your health! We asked five managing directors how they coped.

Their top ten tips for ways of keeping healthy and stress-free are:

- *going* to the gym three times a week.
- _____ sensibly.
- _____ alcohol at lunch.
- _____ work home.
- _____ at least seven hours' sleep each night.
- _____ about business at home.
- _____ mineral water instead of strong coffee.
- _____ a daily 'power nap'.
- _____ to bed after eleven o'clock during the week.
- _____ fattening snacks between meals.

b Complete the second sentence so that it has a similar meaning to the first one, using a gerund.

1   It can be expensive to eat out.
    Eating out can be _____ expensive.

2   I find it easy to make new friends.
    _____ easy for me.

3   I hate it when people drop their rubbish in the street.
    I hate _____ .

4   It can be very stressful when you start a new job.
    _____ very stressful.

5   My mother-in-law can't stand people who smoke when she's eating.
    My mother-in-law _____ .

6   I find that a good way to relax is to have a nice long bath.
    _____ a good way to relax.

Pronunciation
Nouns and verbs which are the same

> LOOK!
>
> Many nouns are the same as verbs:
>
> • an at·tack / to at·tack / re·spect / to re·spect
>
> Usually their pronunciation is the same, but there are some common nouns that change their stress when they become verbs:
>
> • a de·crease – to de·crease
>
> Remember that a dictionary can help you to find where the stress is. This symbol ' means that the stress is on the following syllable:
>
> • /'diːkriːs/ n   /dɪ'kriːs/ v
>
> If a noun and verb are pronounced the same then the pronunciation will be given after the first entry only:
> e.g. control /kən'trəʊl/ n

4 **a** Read the words in phonemic script and mark the stressed syllables on the nouns and verbs in the chart below.

/'diːkriːs/ n	/dɪ'kriːs/ v	/'rekɔːd/ n	/rɪ'kɔːd/ v
/sə'pɔːt/ n	/sə'pɔːt/ v	/'riːsɜːtʃ/ n	/rɪ'sɜːtʃ/ v
/kən'trəʊl/ n	/kən'trəʊl/ v	/'dæmɪdʒ/ n	/'dæmɪdʒ/ v
/'ɪnkriːs/ n	/ɪn'kriːs/ v	/'trænspɔːt/ n	/træn'spɔːt/ v
/'prɒmɪs/ n	/'prɒmɪs/ v	/sə'praɪz/ n	/sə'praɪz/ v
/'ɪmpɔːt/ n	/ɪm'pɔːt/ v	/'ekspɔːt/ n	/ɪk'spɔːt/ v

noun	verb	noun	verb
decrease	decrease	record	record
support	support	research	research
control	control	damage	damage
increase	increase	transport	transport
promise	promise	surprise	surprise
import	import	export	export

b **T2.1** Listen and repeat some of the nouns and verbs in sentences.

Forming adjectives

5 **a** Complete the table below. Then mark the stressed syllables on each word. Use a dictionary if necessary.

noun	adjective	negative adjective
hope	1 _hopeful_	2 _hopeless_
health	3 _____	4 _____
formality	5 _____	6 _____
efficiency	7 _____	8 _____
success	9 _____	10 _____
person	11 _____	12 _____
responsibility	13 _____	14 _____
law	15 _____	16 _____
patience	17 _____	18 _____
honesty	19 _____	20 _____

b **T2.2** Listen and check. Then repeat, paying attention to the stress.

c Choose eight of the adjectives and write sentences to show their meaning.

1 _Mike is very irresponsible, so I would never lend anything to him._

2 _____

3 _____

4 _____

5 _____

6 _____

7 _____

8 _____

Word building with nouns, verbs and adjectives

6 Read the extracts. Then complete the gaps by changing the words in capitals to the correct form.

 A

For years, (a) __psychologists__ have been helping us to understand our dreams. If you go to sleep in an (b) _____ state of mind, you are likely to experience (c) _____ nightmares. A wild animal is likely to symbolise a (d) _____ fear you are trying to avoid. Being chased can indicate outside (e) _____ , particularly from work. Dreaming of death can show either (f) _____ of another or a (g) _____ change in your own life. Losing all your teeth shows you are worried about your (h) _____ with other people. (i) _____ insist that everyone dreams each night, but many of us have no (j) _____ of our dreams when we wake up.	PSYCHOLOGY ANXIETY DISTURB PERSON PRESS ENVIOUS DRAMA RELATE SCIENCE REMEMBER

B

Films which involve a lot of fighting do contribute to (a) _____ among young people, according to recent (b) _____ . Children tended to see killers as 'cool' and (c) '_____', and were so (d) _____ whilst watching, that their heart rate changed significantly. To them, any (e) _____ was not real and they had (f) _____ afterwards of controlling people, using guns. The results are very (g) _____ , since often children cannot distinguish between (h) _____ events and (i) _____ . This has been seen recently in the USA, where after one (j) _____ playground killing, a child said, 'Doctor, I had no idea that bullets could hurt.'	VIOLENT RESEARCH EXCITE INVOLVE SUFFER FANTASTIC WORRY IMAGINE REAL TRAGEDY

Prefixes

7 Find ten words with prefixes in the word square, using the clues to help you.

P	U	R	Y	A	V	E	E	S	G	R	T
U	R	O	S	N	P	O	X	E	P	P	C
N	O	N	S	T	O	P	P	M	R	O	O
D	I	S	A	I	O	U	R	P	O	S	V
E	N	D	O	C	R	E	E	A	D	T	E
R	R	E	P	L	A	Y	F	T	E	G	R
C	R	R	U	O	I	L	L	O	M	R	C
O	V	E	R	C	R	I	I	R	O	A	H
O	R	V	E	K	W	Y	G	T	C	D	A
K	R	E	A	W	A	H	H	Y	R	U	R
E	R	N	I	I	S	T	T	E	A	A	G
D	M	I	S	S	P	E	L	L	C	T	E
S	E	L	F	E	M	P	L	O	Y	E	D

a We've been working __non-stop__ since eight this morning. Let's have a break.

b I'm sorry. I always _____ your name – is it *ie* or *y* at the end?

c Could you _____ that part of the video? I didn't see the goal.

d Excuse me, but I think you have _____ me. I only had a coffee and the bill is for €30!

e Bill's _____ , so he doesn't have a boss and he can choose when he works.

f To open a bottle, you always turn the top in an _____ direction.

g Aung San Suu Kyi led the p _____ movement in Myanmar (Burma).

h The airport has a special _____ departure lounge for VIPs (Very Important Persons).

i After she'd left Oxford University, Emily went on to study as a _____ .

j Waiter! I'm afraid this chicken is _____ .

Real life
Responding sympathetically

8 a Look back at the box on page 23 of the Students' Book and insert a missing word into each response below.

1 A: I'm sorry. I've spilt my coffee all over your tablecloth.
   B: Never *mind* It's easily washable.

2 A: I can't stop thinking about Helen's operation.
   B: There's nothing you can do so try not worry about it.

3 A: The kids at school keep laughing at my hair.
   B: Don't take notice of them.

4 A: I think my boss heard me saying that he annoys me.
   B: He probably didn't hear you. There's point in getting upset about it.

5 A: I've got to have four teeth out tomorrow.
   B: That awful!

6 A: My son is going into hospital for tests next week.
   B: You be really worried.

7 A: I just can't do it! I'm too nervous! Someone else will have to give the speech.
   B: Come on. Pull yourself!

8 A: Andy said my dress makes me look fat!
   B: Just him. You look perfect!

9 A: Our car won't be ready until the weekend.
   B: Annoying!

10 A: I'm so sorry. I completely forgot to bring that book you wanted to borrow.
   B: Don't worry. It doesn't.

b ⬤ T2.3 Listen and check.

Improve your writing
Responding sympathetically in writing

9 **a** Which of these three situations is the letter below responding to?
_____

A

A friend writes to tell you that she's split up with her fiancé and that she's worried because she's in the same class as him at college. Also, she can't concentrate on studying for her exams.

B

A friend writes to tell you that she's lost her job and she's worried that she's too old to find a new job easily, and about the effect that it will have on her family.

C

A friend writes to tell you that she's failed her final exam at university and therefore will not get the job she had been offered. She's worried about telling her family and about paying back the money she borrowed in order to study.

---

25 Cedar Avenue,
Macclesfield,
Cheshire
15th September, 200-

Dear Brigitte,

Thanks for your letter. (1) __I was so sorry to hear your news__ , it was quite a shock because I know how hard you've been studying recently. (2) _____ , especially because of how your family might react — but do you really need to tell them yet? (3) _____ about the job — after all, from what you say, they haven't made a definite decision yet. (4) _____ finances, but I'm sure the bank will understand if you explain the situation.

(5) _____ You'd be welcome to come and stay at my house for a while (6) _____ with your finances. Do keep in touch — give me a ring if you want to talk it over.

love,
Sylvie

---

b Complete the gaps in the letter with the correct phrases from the box.

Is there anything at all I can do?
~~I was so sorry to hear your news~~
if that would help
It sounds like a really difficult situation
Try not to worry too much
I know you must be really worried about

c Write a letter responding to one of the other two situations above. Try to use some of the expressions in the box.

Listen and read
Favourite films

10 ^a **T2.4** Listen to and/or read some people's opinions about films. Which question does each person answer?

In the movies …
1 What makes you cry?
2 What makes you feel good?
3 What makes you scared?

A ___1___   B _____   C _____   D _____

E _____   F _____

 A

In *It's a Wonderful Life* with James Stewart the scene that gets me is at the end when one guy says: 'To my big brother, George, the richest man in town.' It kills me, man. In the film it's Christmas and James Stewart is in big trouble financially and he's going to be arrested and so he decides to kill himself. But then this angel comes down (only he looks like an ordinary guy) and shows him what life would have been like in his home town if he'd never lived. And he sees how his life has touched all these other lives and really made a difference. I watch most of the film with a lump in my throat. Brilliant!

Pete

B

One of the funniest moments I think is in the first *Indiana Jones* movie, *Raiders of the Lost Ark*, when Harrison Ford is trying to escape from his enemies. It takes place in an eastern market and Indiana is suddenly faced by an enormous man wearing a turban and carrying a huge sword. The man gives an awesome display of swordplay with this sword and you can see this feeling of panic passing over Indiana's face. Then he suddenly pulls out a gun and just shoots the guy. The first time I saw it the audience broke out in a cheer. Amazing! Apparently, I read later, they were going to do a full fight but Ford didn't want to spend hours in the scorching sun and it would have been very expensive, so he asked Spielberg (the director) if he could just shoot the guy and Spielberg agreed.

Mel

 C

The opening of *Jaws*. It's all in the music, which is played on the cello. I expect everyone knows it. You start by seeing the sea from the point of view of a shark on the bottom of the sea bed. Then the scene moves to a beach and it's a sunny day and all these families are sunbathing and having a good time. Then there's a girl who goes into the water, and suddenly we're under the water again, looking at the girl's legs from the shark's point of view. Then suddenly she screams and she's dragged across the surface of the water before she disappears. I was on the edge of my seat. It's much more effective than showing the shark straightaway. And for the rest of the film every time that music comes back you know something awful is going to happen.

Lisa

D

Star Wars, every time. Not the later films but the very first film right at the end when Luke Skywalker joins the rebel attack on the Death Star. The Death Star is this huge artificial 'moon' which is about to destroy the rebels' planet. And the only way to destroy it is for the X-wing pilots to fly down a narrow lane and hit a tiny opening. All of Luke's fellow-pilots are killed or their X-wings are damaged and it's up to him alone. He makes the decision to switch off his computer and use 'the Force' to find his target. 'Great shot, kid!' says Han Solo. 'That was one in a million!'

Steve

E

The most I've ever cried in a movie was in *Pay it Forward*. It's about this kid, Trevor, and on his first day of school he gets this assignment 'Think of an idea to change the world, and put it into practice.' And he has this idea that the world would change if everyone did good deeds for three other people, and then those three people would help three other people, and so on, and eventually it would spread right round the world. And then he gets killed trying to help a friend. And they ask everyone who has received an act of kindness or help as a result of his idea to light a candle and you see all these thousands of candles. I tell you, no one had a dry eye in the cinema.

Sandy

F

Jurassic Park. The bit when the two kids are in the jeep and it's broken down and there's some water in the back and you hear this thumping noise and all you see is the movement in the water and the fear in their eyes when they understand what it means. I saw it when I was about eleven and I was petrified. That was more frightening than actually seeing the Tyrannosaurus rex.

Anna

b Listen and/or read again and answer the questions.

Which films …
1 are about someone's positive effect on other people?
_____
2 involve a fight or battle?_____
3 depend a lot on the accompanying music or sound effects? _____

c Are these statements true (T) or false (F)?

1 In *It's a Wonderful Life*, James Stewart has a lot of money. ___F___
2 The angel shows him an alternative future. _____
3 In *Raiders of the Lost Ark*, Indiana Jones is initially afraid of the swordsman. _____
4 The shooting scene had been planned from the start of the film. _____
5 In *Jaws*, you don't see the shark at the beginning. _____
6 In *Star Wars*, Luke hits the target with no help from his computer. _____
7 The boy's idea in *Pay it Forward* is successful. _____
8 The children in *Jurassic Park* only become afraid when they see the dinosaur. _____

Wordspot
life

11 Complete the gaps with a word or phrase with *life* from page 26 of the Students' Book. The phrase is the number of words in brackets. Remember, contractions count as two words, e.g. *I'll = 2 words*.

a A: Are your aunt and uncle rich?
B: Yes, they live _a life of luxury_ . (4 words)
b A: Is he enjoying himself in Nigeria?
B: Yes, he's having _____ . (5 words)
c A: What a brilliant statue. It looks just like her.
B: Yes, it's very _____ . (1 word)
d A: What will Taylor get for blowing up the hotel?
B: Probably a _____ . He'll be in prison for a long time. (2 words)
e A: I've been offered a top job at NASA.
B: Wow! That's the _____ . Lucky you! (4 words)
f A: Are you enjoying college?
B: Yes, the work's quite hard but I have a good _____ . Lots of parties! (2 words)
g A: Did you get a good interview with her?
B: Yes, but she refused to answer questions about her _____ . (2 words)
h A: You won't believe who I saw getting into her car the other day! Jennifer Aniston!
B: Really? What does she look like _____ ? (3 words)
i A: I'm sorry you didn't get the job in Paris.
B: Yes, I was very disappointed, but _____ ! I really wasn't sure I wanted to move to France anyway. (3 words)
j A: Should we put our _____ on now? (1 word)
B: No, wait until you get on board the yacht.
k A: So you're working with your ex-girlfriend?
B: Yes, and it's _____ very difficult for me. (2 words)
l A: Amy looks very well.
B: Yes, she's working as a _____ at the outdoor swimming pool, and really enjoying it. (1 word)

Vocabulary
Mishaps

1 **a** Read these extracts from www.myworststory.com and replace the words or phrases in bold with a better word or phrase from page 29 of the Students' Book.

Back Forward Stop Refresh Home Favorites History Search AutoFill Larger Smaller Print Mail Preferences

myworststory.com

My worst wedding story

It was my friend Mike's wedding and it was in a church in the middle of nowhere about 40 km from Vancouver. Anyway I didn't have a map and I (1) **became unable to find my way** and missed the ceremony. Then at the party afterwards I (2) **hit my foot and almost fell** and (3) **dropped from my glass** red wine all over the bride's wedding dress! Worst of all, at the end of an uncomfortable evening I realized I (4) **was unable to find** the piece of paper with the name of my hotel and so I had to sleep in my car.
Steve - Canada

1 _____got lost_____   2 _____   3 _____   4 _____

My worst interview story

I had an interview for a job I really wanted. Unfortunately, my alarm clock didn't go off and I (5) **slept too much**. I rushed to the station but I was in such a state that I (6) **entered** the wrong train. I didn't arrive in Frankfurt until lunchtime and I was three hours (7) **behind time for** the interview. Needless to say, I didn't get the job.
Helga - Germany

5 _____   6 _____   7 _____

My worst journey story

I'd just been to a terrible party in Edinburgh and it was January. Well, on my way home, my car (8) **stopped working** and I (9) **hadn't brought my mobile from home**, so I had to walk. It had been snowing and the road was very icy and I (10) **slid with my feet** on the ice and (11) **knocked my head hard** on a tree. I woke up later in hospital with a very bad headache.
Pat - Scotland

8 _____   9 _____   10 _____   11 _____

My worst car story

... happened when I had to catch a plane from Madrid. I started off nice and early but then on the way there I (12) **used all my petrol and didn't have any left**. I managed to buy a can from a nearby garage, but when I got back to the car I saw my keys inside it and realized I had (13) **kept myself out by locking it**. A helpful mechanic from the garage found a key that opened the door and I continued on my journey. As I approached Madrid I (14) **became unable to move** in traffic for half an hour. As you can imagine, I (15) **failed to catch** my plane.
José - Spain

12 _____   13 _____   14 _____   15 _____

b Complete the gaps with a word or phrase from part a, making any necessary changes to the verbs.

1 Hello, is that Park Street Garage? My car _has broken down_. Can you send someone to help?

2 Be careful or you _____ your coffee!

3 Eric _____ most of the meeting. He only arrived fifteen minutes before the end.

4 A: What happened?
  B: The floor was wet and I _____ and twisted my ankle. It's nothing serious.

5 You _____ the wrong train. This one is going to London. The Birmingham train is on platform nine.

6 The city centre is terrible. You can _____ in traffic jams for hours.

7 The hotel was so large that the first day Haifa worked there she _____ and ended up in the laundry room.

8 Sorry to bother you but I _____ sugar. Can you lend me some?

9 If you don't hurry you _____ work. It's already eight-thirty.

10 I'm sorry I'm so late. My neighbours kept me awake last night and I _____ this morning.

11 Oh no! I _____ my football bag at home. I'm going to have to go back for it.

12 A: Are you okay?
   B: Yes, I just _____ my head on the cupboard door. I think I need to sit down for a moment.

13 It was dark in the living room and the police officer _____ over something and nearly fell.

14 She closed the door and then realised she _____ . Her key was still inside.

15 _____ anybody _____ a wallet? I found this in the hall.

c T3.1 Listen and check.

Reading
A short break in Copenhagen

2 a Before you read the extract on the opposite page from a travel brochure, write down two things you know about Copenhagen.

1 _____
_____

2 _____
_____

b Read the text and answer these questions to a travel agent.

1 Is it necessary to hire a car while we're there?

_____ .

2 My son says that you can visit the place where Carlsberg beer is made. Is that true?

_____ .

3 Where's the best place to go shopping?

_____ .

4 I don't want to stay in a big hotel, I find them too impersonal. Which one do you suggest?

_____ .

5 I'd like to stay in a hotel near the harbour. Where do you recommend?

_____ .

6 I'd like to visit the castle where *Hamlet* is set. Is that possible on a Saturday in March?

_____ .

7 How much would it cost to stay in the cheapest hotel for two nights in October?

_____ .

8 How much is a taxi from the airport to the city centre and how long does it take?

_____ .

Copenhagen

Although capital of one of Europe's smallest countries, the clean and friendly city of Copenhagen offers a host of cultural and sightseeing opportunities. With a vast number of pedestrianised streets, the best way to sightsee is by foot, or you may prefer a leisurely canal cruise past the colourful waterfront houses.

Sights not to be missed include Rosenborg Castle which houses the Crown Jewels, Amalienborg Palace, the Little Mermaid and, of course, the famous Tivoli Gardens with a myriad of restaurants and bars, concert halls and a fairground offering something for everyone. Also worth a visit is the Viking Museum, and for something different why not tour the Carlsberg Brewery?

Shoppers will enjoy the fine shops of the Stroget, and don't forget the side-streets leading from it. After sunset head for Nyhavn quayside.

My comment:

"A rarity among capital cities – it does not overwhelm you, but rather takes you gently in and shows you its sights with quiet pride. The Little Mermaid is smaller than you imagined (but she is, after all, 'Little') and there isn't a single inch of neon among the light bulbs of Tivoli."

John Carter

1 HOTEL MAYFAIR
This comfortable hotel is located in the heart of the city, just a few minutes from Tivoli Gardens.

Breakfast room ◆ bar ◆ 102 English-style rooms with en suite facilities, colour television, hairdryer, mini bar and telephone

2 HOTEL SAVOY
Copenhagen's many attractions are all within easy reach of this small, friendly hotel.

Breakfast room ◆ courtyard café ◆ bar ◆ 66 rooms with private facilities, colour television, mini bar, radio and telephone

3 HOTEL ADMIRAL
A characteristic hotel within a half-timbered building, ideally situated in the centre of Copenhagen close to the Royal Palace, Theatre and the harbour.

Restaurant ◆ bar ◆ nightclub ◆ 363 rooms with en suite facilities, colour television, hairdryer and telephone

PRICES are in £s per person, sharing a twin / double room, departing from GATWICK with BRITISH AIRWAYS.									
Hotel Name	Savoy			Mayfair			Admiral		
Holiday No	10802			10800			10804		
No of Nights in hotel	1	2	Extra Night	1	2	Extra Night	1	2	Extra Night
01 Jan – 13 Apr	238	269	31	249	291	42	245	285	38
14 Apr – 29 Apr	238	269	31	249	291	42	266	326	60
30 Apr – 30 Sep	252	298	45	252	298	45	266	326	60
01 Oct – 31 Oct	239	273	32	251	295	44	266	326	60
01 Nov – 31 Dec	239	273	32	251	295	44	247	289	40
Single Supp (per night)	26			30			41		

HOTEL INFORMATION – Mon–Thur supplements (in £s per adult, per night):–
Admiral – 01 Jan – 02 Apr & 01 Nov – 11 Dec – £21 in a twin/double or £38 in a single
Mayfair – 01 May – 30 Sep – £7 in a twin/double or £13 in a single
Superior room supplements (in £s per adult, per night) – Mayfair – £14 in a twin/double or a single;
(except Mon–Thur between 30 Apr – 30 Sep – £20 in a twin/double; £26 in a single.)

ALTERNATIVE HOTELS
Premier Holidays are able to offer additional hotels in Copenhagen – please ask for details.

ONE OR TWO NIGHT STAYS – must include a Saturday night

TRANSFER OPTIONS – Transfers between the airport and your hotel are not included.
As a guide we have listed examples of the public transport available:–
AIRPORT/CITY – Airport Shuttle bus to city centre – 20 kroner; journey – 20 mins;
Taxi – 160 kroner; journey – 15 mins

PRE-BOOKABLE EXCURSIONS

CITY & HARBOUR TOUR – £18
This 2½ hour tour begins with a coach tour passing Tivoli Gardens, New Carlsberg Glypotek and the Gefion Fountain, then by boat past the Little Mermaid and along the picturesque canals to Christianshavn.
DEPARTS – Daily between 13 Jun – 13 Sep

CASTLE TOUR OF NORTH SEALAND – £37
A full day tour which includes a visit to Kronborg Castle – the setting for Shakespeare's *Hamlet* – and Fredensborg Castle which is the Queen's summer residence.
DEPARTS – Weds & Sun – 01 Jan – 29 Apr & 17 Oct – 31 Dec; Wed, Sat & Sun 02 May – 16 Oct

Past simple, Past continuous and Past perfect in narrative

3 a Use the prompts to write complete sentences. Choose the best past form of the verbs.

1

This / happen / one summer when three of us / travel / around Europe.

This happened one summer ...

_____

_____

_____ .

2

We / walk / around a town when a man / offer / to change our money.

_____

_____

_____ .

3

A friend / warn / us never to change money on the street, but the man / look / honest, so we / decide / to take a chance.

_____

_____

_____ .

4

He / pretend / to give me fifty notes but I / notice / that he / only give / me forty-eight, so I / ask / him to count them again.

_____

_____

_____ .

5

Ten minutes later we / sit / in a café when I / realise / that he / trick / us.

_____

_____

_____ .

6

When he / give / me back the money, he / replace / everything except the top two notes with newspaper!

_____

_____

_____ .

b ⬛**T3.2** Underline the words you think should be stressed in the completed story in part a. Listen and check.

Past perfect simple or continuous

4 Choose the best verb form in the sentences.

a I couldn't believe that my brother ⟨had sold⟩ / had been selling his bike.

b I could see immediately that Frank *had drunk / had been drinking*.

c The Minister of Transport, Carole Whitaker, told journalists that she *had resigned / had been resigning* from her job.

d Carmen and Nando *had gone out / had been going out* for several years, so we were shocked when they split up.

e The children were disappointed because Chris *hadn't come / hadn't been coming* to their party.

f Kate was exhausted because she *'d worked / 'd been working* so hard.

g I felt extremely frustrated, as I *'d tried / 'd been trying* to telephone his office for three days, with no success.

h It was only when I got home that I realised, to my horror, that I *hadn't paid / hadn't been paying* for the meal.

Past simple/continuous and Past perfect simple/continuous in narrative

5 These letters about life's biggest disappointments were sent to a teen magazine. Complete the gaps with the correct form of the verbs in the boxes.

Liz, aged twelve

My sister (a) ___cancelled___ her wedding three days before it was due to happen. I (b) _____ to make her change her mind because I (c) _____ to wearing the dress that my mum (d) _____ for me for weeks. On the day she was supposed to get married I (e) _____ into her room while she (f) _____ a bath and (g) _____ her favourite dress into little pieces.

---

try	go	cut	make	~~cancel~~	look forward	have

Joseph, aged eleven

My dad is always playing practical jokes on us, and the worst one ever was the lottery one. We (h) _____ the lottery for years and we (i) _____ anything, so when my dad (j) _____ us a lottery ticket with the winning numbers from that night on it, we (k) _____ believe our luck! Later, when we (l) _____ what to spend the money on, he (m) _____ us the ticket was a fake he (n) _____ . My mum (o) _____ to him for weeks!

---

show	not win	tell	not speak	do	can't	plan	make

Listen and read
Winners and losers

6 **a** **T3.3** Listen to and/or read about three unlucky experiences and answer the question.

Who lost the most money?

_____

b Listen to or read the texts again. Are these statements true (T) or false (F)?

1 Mrs Song gave the teddy bear to the sale by mistake. _____

2 There were plenty of objects for sale at the jumble sale. _____

3 The syndicate members didn't take the robbery seriously at first. _____

4 The party was only for the syndicate members. _____

5 Eric Culbertson was going to propose in a hotel. _____

6 The couple are now engaged. _____

c Who made the following statements?

1 'They seemed very pleased with it.' _The person who sold the_ _teddy at the jumble sale._

2 'Yes, I will.' _____

3 'It's devastating but we shall just have to try again.'

_____

4 'She should have told me.'

_____

5 'It's just sad to work that hard, to plan all that, then to have it all ruined.' _____

6 'They were rather foolish to let everyone know what was going to happen.' _____

7 'I told nobody at first, then decided that the buyer is more likely to return the money if they know who it belongs to.'

_____

8 'Nobody move!' _____

Family accidentally sold teddy bear containing $50,000 in cash

An Alaskan family accidentally sold an old teddy bear containing $50,000 in cash at a church jumble sale. Wan Song had borrowed the money for her husband's cancer treatment and had hidden it inside the bear. But she hadn't told her husband, Inhong Song, who gave the bear to the church sale in their home town of Anchorage.

Mrs Song is now appealing for whoever bought the bear to return it to the family. She had borrowed the money from friends and relatives without her husband's knowledge, to pay for surgery he needed for cancer of the pancreas.

For safekeeping, she wrapped the money in foil and sewed it inside one of their children's old teddy bears which she then hid at the back of a cupboard. Meanwhile, the family decided to help their local church jumble sale and Mrs Song packed up some items which her husband delivered.

But when the jumble sale began to run out of items, he went back to the house, found the bear and brought it to the sale.

An older woman with two girls reportedly bought it for a dollar.

Lottery syndicate robbed of winnings at celebration party

An Italian lottery syndicate won and then lost a fortune when members were robbed at gunpoint as they divided up their $60,000 winnings. Five masked gunmen burst into the celebration party at a social club as the money was being handed out in envelopes, and grabbed the cash before escaping in a waiting car.

Syndicate organiser Vincenzo Paviglianiti said: 'We were just about to start handing out the money when five men burst in wearing masks. At first everyone laughed because they thought it was part of the party but then the men started shouting and telling everyone to get on the floor and not to move. It was only after one of them fired a shot into the air that everyone realised it wasn't a joke. They took all the money, but at least no one was hurt.'

Police said the forty-strong syndicate may have been the victim of its own generosity after advertising the party on posters at Reggio Calabria in southern Italy. A spokesman said: 'The syndicate had put up posters and balloons in the streets around their local social club and had invited neighbours to come and celebrate their win with them. In effect the robbers knew what was going to happen and that the money was going to be divided up at the celebration.'

Man loses $10,000 engagement ring in taxi

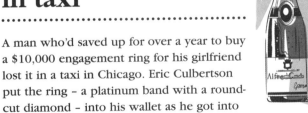

A man who'd saved up for over a year to buy a $10,000 engagement ring for his girlfriend lost it in a taxi in Chicago. Eric Culbertson put the ring – a platinum band with a round-cut diamond – into his wallet as he got into the taxi. He was taking girlfriend Krista Saputo to a restaurant where he'd intended to propose. But after leaving the taxi he realised the ring was no longer in his wallet.

The twenty-eight-year-old had paid for a suite at a city hotel and arranged for chocolate-covered strawberries and champagne for their arrival. He'd also booked a table at a restaurant in the city, says the *Chicago Tribune*.

The following day the couple travelled to Pleasant Prairie, Wisconsin for a family reunion. There, Culbertson bought a twenty-five-dollar cubic zirconia ring and asked Saputo to marry him. She accepted.

Improve your writing
Useful phrases for narratives

7 **a** Read Marisol's story and make sure you understand what happened.

The Most Frightening Experience of My Life

One of the most frightening experiences
of my life happened while

∧ I was spending Christmas in Tenerife, in the Canary Islands. My brother José was working there and he couldn't get any time off to come home, so I spent the holiday with him. We decided to go up Mt. Teide, a volcano in the centre of the island, and officially the second largest mountain in Europe. We hired a little car for the day – I couldn't drive, but my brother could.

José and I set off in brilliant sunshine, but it got much colder and by the time we reached the crater of Mt. Teide it was snowing. All the restaurants, hotels and petrol stations at the top of the volcano were shut, and we had almost run out of petrol. I was really worried because I had to catch the plane home that evening, and if I didn't,

I would have to pay for a new ticket. José decided to do something incredibly dangerous – he switched off the engine of the car and freewheeled down the other side of the mountain. He did this for several kilometres, round hairpin bends on dangerous icy roads. I was absolutely petrified, but for some reason I didn't tell him to stop.

The car slipped on the road and the two front wheels went over the edge. We were very lucky that the rest of the car didn't go over. We sat in the car, not daring to move and freezing cold, waiting for someone to come past. Then suddenly a car came round the corner and out jumped three enormous men. The three men surrounded the car and literally lifted it back on the road. My brother and I got out to thank them, but the three men just repeated 'Norway' several times – we assumed that that was where they came from – then got back into their car and drove off. We got back into our car and continued down the side of the mountain. I have never felt so happy in my life as when we reached the town – and the petrol station – at the bottom.

b Improve the story by inserting these phrases in the best place. They are in the correct order.

~~One of the most frightening experiences of my life happened while~~   unfortunately   On the last day of my visit
before long   What is more,   As you can imagine,   So   Then my worst nightmare happened:
for about half an hour   Without saying a word,   With great relief,

c Look back at the story you wrote about a frightening experience (page 36 of the Students' Book). Can you add any of the phrases above to improve your story?

Present perfect simple or continuous

8 Complete the extract with the Present perfect simple or continuous of the verbs in brackets.

Shridhar Chillal, who lives near Bombay, (a) _____ *has been* _____ (be) in the *Guinness Book of Records* for the last twenty years for having the world's longest nails (one is more than a hundred centimetres long). He (b) _____ (grow) them for more than fifty years and has to be extremely careful in case he damages them. However, recently he (c) _____ (feel) very tired: 'My nails are very heavy and I (d) _____ (not had) a full night's sleep for the last few years, worrying about damaging them. I (e) _____ (never hold) my new grandson for fear of breaking them, and now the nerves in my left hand (f) _____ (die) because I (g) _____ (never use) it. I (h) _____ (think) about it a lot recently and now I (i) _____ (decide) to cut off my nails and sell them to a museum.'

Future simple or continuous

9 Complete the e-mail with the Future simple or continuous form of the verbs in the box.

| be | bring | have | look after | not forget | not work | ~~pack~~ |
| phone | send | wander |

Message

Reply   Reply All   Forward   🖨 📁 ✖ ⇧ ⇩   Follow Up A ▾

Hi Julian,

Just a quick e-mail before we go away. We're off to Morocco tomorrow. I can't wait, but I'm nowhere near ready yet. I think I (a) _'ll be packing_ all night! I'm sure by the time I get on the plane I (b) _____ exhausted!

Still, just think, this time next week I (c) _____ round the old city or maybe I (d) _____ a swim in the hotel pool. The great thing is I (e) _____! I promise I (f) _____ you a postcard and I (g) _____ you something back from Marrakech.

As I said, Sandra (h) _____ Tigger from Monday to Friday but if you could feed him on Saturday and Sunday, that would be brilliant. You (i) _____ to give him some milk as well, will you?

Thanks again and I (j) _____ you as soon as we get back.
Trish
xx

Real life
Dealing with unexpected problems

10 **a** Complete the phrases with words from page 38 of the Students' Book.

1 A: I'm afraid we don't have those shoes in a size 6.
   B: Oh, _dear_ .

2 Is your birthday dinner next Tuesday? Oh what _____ . I'd have loved to come, but I'm away on a business trip.

3 A: I'm sorry, we're just closing.
   B: Oh no! You _____ ! It's only ten to five! I have to post this parcel today.

4 I can't find my glasses. This is _____ ! I only had them five minutes ago.

5 Oh, for _____ sake! Why can't they have machines that give you change! We're going to miss our train!

6 A: Two tickets for Saturday? I'm sorry, we've sold out.
   B: Oh, that's _____ .

7 A: Mum, can I go to the cinema on Friday evening?
   B: I don't see _____ .

8 I don't _____ ! I've got a parking ticket! But we're only five minutes late.

b **T3.4** Listen and check.

Pronunciation
Contractions and weak forms

11 **a** **T3.5** Listen to six answerphone messages and write them in the spaces below. Remember, contractions count as two words, e.g. _I'll = 2 words._

1 Daniel here – _I'll be working late tonight so don't wait up for me_ . (13 words)

2 This is Helen – _____
   _____
   _____
   _____ . (18 words)

3 It's Peter Crawford – _____
   _____
   _____
   _____ . (19 words)

4 This is Jenny McAdam – _____
   _____
   _____
   _____
   _____ . (20 words)

5 Anna, it's Roger – _____
   _____
   _____
   _____ . (15 words)

6 This is Simpson's Fabric Department – _____
   _____
   _____
   _____ . (12 words)

b Listen again and repeat the sentences, paying attention to stress and contracted and weak forms.

Vocabulary
Qualities of mind

1 Complete the grid with adjectives to describe the people speaking in the clues below. All the words can be found in the box on page 41 of the Students' Book.

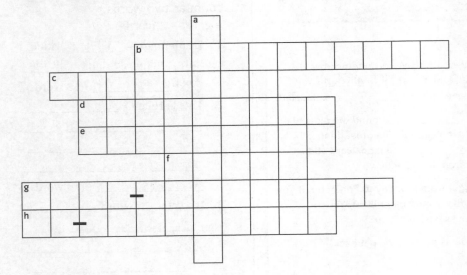

a 'I always cry during movies, even if they're happy ones!'

b 'I was so sorry to hear about your exam results. I'm sure you'll do better next time.'

c 'No, I refuse to apologise. I don't care what any of you think!'

d 'I've done all the plumbing and electrical work on the house myself.'

e 'I had a very bad feeling about Susan when I first met her, so I wasn't at all surprised to find out she'd been in trouble with the police.'

f 'Jo, you be the daddy. I'll be the mummy. And Tim, you have to sit here.'

g 'I'm looking forward to my exams. I think I'm going to do really well.'

h 'Yes, of course, officer. I'll do whatever you want me to.'

Pronunciation
Stress patterns

2 **a** Put the words from the grid in 1 under the correct stress pattern.

● ● ● ●	● ● ● ● ●	● ● ● ●
emotional		
● ●	● ● ●	

b T4.1 Listen and repeat the words, paying attention to the stress.

Listen and read

3 **a** Write down: two adjectives to describe male drivers _____ _____ and two adjectives to describe female drivers _____ _____ .

b T4.2 Listen to and/or read the article. Put a tick (✓) next to the things you agree with.

c According to the article, are these statements true (T) or false (F)?

1 The woman was driving the wrong way down the motorway. __T__

2 The father thought he was better than other drivers. ____

3 Cathy does nearly all the driving in her family. ____

4 Cathy thinks men overtake other cars in order to reach their destination quicker. ____

5 Danielle thinks men are not very considerate of other drivers. ____

6 Older men are probably more popular with insurance companies than young men. ____

7 Paul seems to be a very careful driver. ____

8 Pete thinks men are better than women at following directions to somewhere new. ____

9 Many men think it's not their fault if they get directions wrong. ____

10 Pete's girlfriend sometimes uses the wrong lever when she's signalling. ____

11 She also brakes too much when going round a corner. ____

12 Men are better at parking than women. ____

Driving Each Other Crazy

There's a well-known joke: a woman is driving down a motorway and her husband phones her on her mobile. 'Darling, be careful!' he screams, 'I've just heard there's a car driving the wrong way on the motorway near where you are.' 'It's not just one car,' she says, 'there are hundreds of them!'

And here's another one: a man is driving his daughter and they are stuck in traffic. The little girl says, 'I have a question.' 'What is it?' asks her father. 'When you're driving, are YOU ever the stupid idiot?'

Why do we laugh at these jokes? Is it because we recognise some truth in them? A lot of people seem to think that men and women do display quite different characteristics when it comes to driving, and in general, both male and female drivers tend to be quite critical of the opposite sex.

'Men are too confident in their own abilities. They never listen, they never need a map. They're always sure they know the way,' says Cathy, whose husband rarely lets her drive the car. 'They tend to drive too close to the car in front and they're incredibly impatient. If there's a car in front they have to pass it even if it doesn't make a difference to their overall speed. I think it's some sort of territorial thing – you know, they have to be king of the road and everybody else on the road is an idiot.'

Danielle, a businesswoman who drives a BMW, agrees: 'Men never indicate before they turn left and they tend to brake at the very last minute. If I'm in a car with a man, I often feel quite nervous. I'd much rather be driven by a woman.'

It seems as if insurance companies would agree. Apparently, whilst the number of accidents men and women have tend to be about equal, the accidents which involve women are generally relatively minor and they are therefore less expensive to insure. In contrast, men tend to have more serious accidents, and the worst offenders are young men, aged between eighteen and twenty-five.

What do men think about women? Interestingly, one of their main concerns is about women as passengers: 'Women passengers can't keep quiet,' says Paul, a retired architect. 'You know: "You're going too fast", "Can you see that pedestrian?", "Didn't you see that traffic light?" or "I feel sick. Can't you go straight?" There's always some comment.'

Pete agrees: 'And women are hopeless with directions. I think it's because they're nervous about going to new places. I reckon men are better at finding new places and women are better at finding places they've been to before.'

Certainly it seems to be the case that if a man fails to follow directions it's because his female passenger did not convey them properly. But what about women's driving? Pete again: 'My girlfriend has some strange habits, like switching on the windscreen wipers as a signal that she intends to turn right. Then she gets annoyed when she's driving and I 'brake' – you know, put my foot down as if I'm braking – when she's going round corners. I mean, one of us has to!'

Despite men's generally high opinion of their own driving skills, a report published in 2004 came down firmly in favour of women drivers. According to the report, women score more highly than men on almost all counts. These included driving within the speed limits, overtaking safely, and conducting different manoeuvres successfully, including signalling in good time, reversing and braking quickly. They also had a better awareness of other drivers on the road. There was only one aspect of driving where women did not perform as successfully as men and that was (no surprise here) the ability to park their cars.

When it comes to driving, it seems that men and women may indeed come from different planets!

Vocabulary booster
More qualities of mind

4 a Megan is Personnel Officer in a busy hospital. She has just interviewed five people for the position of Senior Nurse. Read her notes and write two adjectives from the box next to each candidate.

bright	~~cheerful~~	conceited	controlling	critical	defensive
indecisive	sensible	sincere	vain		

SARAH: I liked her because she seemed very friendly and positive; she smiled a lot during the interview. The only problem was that she found it difficult to make up her mind when I asked her about different situations she could face.

cheerful _____

JUAN: At first I thought what a nice man - seemed very intelligent but then when I asked him why he'd left his last job and if he had had any problems he got quite angry. We can't have someone who can't take criticism.

_____ _____

MARIA: Very practical and down to earth and no silly answers to my questions. Very honest in her answers and genuinely seems to like her work.

_____ _____

LAURA: No. She seemed to think we should be begging her to join us ... a big ego! I didn't like the way she kept looking at herself in the mirror, either!

_____ _____

JIM: I think he'd be a problem because he wants to be in charge all the time - do everything his way. And he admitted that he thinks it's a good idea to tell colleagues their bad points so they can 'learn!'

_____ _____

b T4.3 Listen and check. Then listen and mark the stressed syllable.

c Complete these sentences so that they are true for you, using six of the adjectives from the box and giving examples.

1 I think I'm quite _cheerful_ _because I'm usually in a good_ _mood and I'm generally_ _optimistic._

I think I'm quite _____
_____
_____
_____
_____ .

2 I'm not at all _____
_____
_____
_____ .

3 I'm sometimes _____
_____
_____
_____ .

4 I tend to be rather _____
_____
_____
_____ .

5 People say I'm _____
_____
_____
_____ .

6 I can't stand people who are
_____
_____
_____
_____ .

Passives

5 **a** Read the clues and find the answer.

1 It's picked.
It's drunk.
It's sometimes sweetened,
but it's never roasted.

What is it? _____ tea _____

2 It was built by a king to show his love for his dead wife.
It's visited by thousands of people every year.
It's made of white stone.
It's been called the most beautiful building in the world.

What is it? _____

3 It's looked at but never read.
It's switched on and off.
It's been blamed for the death of conversation.
It was invented by Logie Baird.

What is it? _____

4 The world's oceans are moved by it daily.
One day cities will be built there.
Mythical stories will always be told about it.
It was first visited in 1969.

What is it? _____

5 She was photographed.
She was sometimes criticised.
She was killed in a car crash.
She was called the people's Princess.

Who was she? _____

6 It's been ruled by kings.
It's been invaded many times.
Its political system was transformed in 1989.
It's surrounded by Germany, the Czech Republic, Slovakia,
Ukraine, Belarus, Lithuania, Russia and the Baltic Sea.

Where is it? _____

b Think of some places, people or things and write clues like the ones
above, using the passive. Then test your classmates.

6 **a** Complete the sentences with the correct passive form of the verbs in brackets, and underline the correct answer.

1 Several famous pictures of waterlilies _were painted_ (paint) by
   (a) Renoir.   (b) <u>Monet</u>.

2 Portuguese _____ (speak) in
   (a) Chile.   (b) Brazil.

3 The structure of DNA _____ (know) about for more than
   (a) thirty years.   (b) fifty years.

4 (a) Meteors   (b) Asteroids
   _____ (study) at the moment in case one hits this planet.

5 New Zealand _____ originally _____ (inhabit) by
   (a) Aborigines.   (b) Maoris.

6 The 2016 Olympics _____ (not hold) in
   (a) China.   (b) India.

7 The Vietnamese war _____ still _____ (fight) in
   (a) 1957.   (b) 1967.

8 The part of Rachel in the American sitcom *Friends* which ran from 1994–2004 _____ (play) by
   (a) Lisa Kudrow.   (b) Jennifer Aniston.

b `T4.4` Listen and check.

C

Licorice (1) _____ (use) by mankind for thousands of years. In China in 3000 BC, licorice

(2) _____ (believe) to have amazing powers and (3) _____ (use) in certain religious ceremonies. People (4) _____ (believe) that it could (5) _____ (protect) the dead from evil spirits.

7 Complete the extracts with the correct active or passive form of the verbs in brackets.

A

Adfen Plus (1) ___ is recommended ___ (recommend) for those times when you (2) _____ (need) powerful relief from pain. The tablets (3) _____ (specially / formulate) to make them easy to swallow. Each tablet (4) _____ (contain) ibuprofen BP 200 mg and aspirin. As with other pain relievers, Adfen Plus should (5) _____ (not / take) if you have any stomach disorders.

B

This little-known castle (1) _____ (only recently / open) its doors to the public, and Qualtours (2) _____ (offer) special reductions for this month only. The tour (3) _____ (include) the living quarters, the library, the kitchens and the gardens. The size of each tour (4) _____ (limit) to twelve people. Bookings may (5) _____ (make) in advance by telephone.

D

An outbreak of food poisoning at a top London hotel (1) _____ (investigate) last night. More than fifteen guests at a business lunch at the Stanmore Hotel (2) _____ (complain) of nausea during the afternoon, after eating shellfish which doctors later found (3) _____ (not / properly / clean). Ten people (4) _____ (currently / treat) in hospital, but most of them expect (5) _____ (send) home later today.

Choosing active or passive

LOOK!

Look at this sentence:

Walt Disney pioneered full-length cartoons.

Which sentence follows best, **a** or **b**?

a *Snow White was made by him in 1937.*
b *He made Snow White in 1937.* ✓

b is the right answer because we are more interested in the **topic** of Walt Disney, so we make him the **subject** of the second sentence.

8 Tick (✓) the best way of continuing after each sentence.

a A man has been arrested for hooliganism.
  1 He is being held in Dundee police station. ✓
  2 They are holding him in Dundee police station.

b Kirk Blane, the controversial rock star, died last night.
  1 An overdose of sleeping pills was taken by him.
  2 He took an overdose of sleeping pills.

c *Night of Passion* has won first prize at the Cannes Film Festival this year.
  1 It was directed by Henrietta Calvin.
  2 Henrietta Calvin directed it.

d How much is breakfast?
  1 It's included in the price.
  2 We include it in the price.

e A man was attacked outside a local pub last night.
  1 He was shot in the chest.
  2 Someone shot him in the chest.

f Alan Curtis has been appointed as Managing Director of Comco.
  1 He will be paid a salary of over $500,000.
  2 A salary of over $500,000 will be paid to him.

g My brother-in-law is very rich.
  1 A house in Barbados has just been bought by him.
  2 He has just bought a house in Barbados.

Formal and conversational use

9 **a** Rewrite the sentences so that they are more formal.

1 Scientists think that if you eat less you are likely to live longer.
  It is thought that if you eat less you are likely to live longer.

2 Scientists have proved that chewing gum can improve your short and long-term memory.
  It _____ .

3 Some people believe that drinking a little red wine daily is good for your health.
  It _____ .

4 People have suggested that taking vitamins reduces violent behaviour.
  It _____ .

5 We know that happy people recover from illnesses more quickly.
  It _____ .

b Rewrite the sentences so that they are more conversational.

1 It is often said that drinking tea reduces stress.
  People often say that drinking tea reduces stress.

2 People's immune systems can be strengthened by taking regular cold showers.
  You _____ .

3 It is known that an Italian diet rich in olive oil, fruit, vegetables and fish can improve the health of people with heart problems.
  We _____ .

4 It is believed that aspirin may reduce the risk of cancer.
  Some people _____ .

5 It has been suggested that chocolate can help people with coughs.
  Someone _____ .

Improve your writing
A formal letter of apology

10 **a** Look back at the letter of complaint on page 46 in the Students' Book. Read this letter of apology from David Martin. Which complaints does he accept and apologise for? Which complaints does he not agree with?

BrainBoost
PO Box 327861

12 January

Dear Mr Mortimer

I am writing *for I / on behalf of* BrainBoost *in relation to / because of* your recent complaint. I was *concerned / upset* to learn about your *dissatisfaction / anger* with certain aspects of our product and service.

In the first instance, *please accept my apologies / I'm sorry* for the late arrival of your BrainBoost package. At the time of your order *we were experiencing / we had* a temporary problem with our delivery service, which has now been rectified. I apologise again, and to *make it better / compensate for the inconvenience caused*, we are refunding the postage and packing charges and, *to be friendly / as a gesture of goodwill*, are sending you a further package of vitamins and minerals.

I am sorry / I am afraid to hear that you feel the BrainBoost exercises are not working for you. I can only reiterate that hundreds of satisfied clients have found them effective and enjoyable. *As regards / Talking about* the vitamins and minerals, I *promise you / can assure you* that our product is superior in quality to similar products found in supermarkets and chemists and that you will notice a difference in your mental abilities if you follow the BrainBoost course.

I apologise again for any inconvenience *caused by / made by* the late delivery of your 'special package.' If you have any *further / extra* queries, please do not *hesitate / wait* to contact me.

Yours sincerely,

David Martin

David Martin
Manager
BrainBoost

---

b We use a number of fixed phrases in a letter of apology. Circle the best alternative in the letter above.

c Look back at your letter of complaint to the company selling the language course (see page 46 of the Students' Book). Write a letter of apology from the company. Try to use at least eight of the expressions above.

Have/get something done

11 **a** Put the words in order to make questions, and write answers which are true for you.

1 your / often / do / have / How / serviced / you / car?
   How often do you have your car serviced?
   Once a year.

2 ever / fortune / your / told / had / you / Have?
   _____
   _____
   _____

3 last / When / your / checked / did / get / teeth / you?
   _____
   _____
   _____

4 have / you / Would / tattooed / ever / a / of / your / part / body?
   _____
   _____
   _____

5 next / you / tested / When / are / having / eyes / your?
   _____
   _____
   _____

6 to / hair / differently / like / have / you / your / cut / Would?
   _____
   _____
   _____

b Complete the dialogues using the correct form of *have* or *get* with the verbs in the box.

clean	~~cut~~	develop	print	put up	repair

1 A: You look different. Have you ___had___ your
      hair ___cut___ ?

   B: Yes. What do you think?

2 A: I'd like to _____ these photos
      _____ quickly.

   B: We can do it in an hour but it's more expensive.

3 A: Can you _____ these business cards
      _____ for me?

   B: Yes, when do you want them done by?

4 A: Oh no! I'm so sorry – all over your shirt!

   B: It really doesn't matter.

   A: No, I'll pay for you to _____ it
      _____ .

5 A: I'm sorry about the noise.

   B: Yes, what's going on?

   A: We _____ some new shelves _____ .

6 A: Oh no, my watch has stopped.

   B: You'd better _____ it _____ .

c ⬤T4.5⬤ Listen and check.

d Listen again and repeat the dialogues, paying
attention to the main stress in each sentence.

Wordspot
mind

12 Insert a missing word from the box into each
sentence below.

absent-	helping	her	in	never	off	on	to
open-	own	speaks	the	up	went	~~don't~~	

    don't

a   I̸ mind doing the cooking if you do the washing-up.

b   She's very tolerant. She's quite minded about things.

c   I'm sorry. I'm not very good company this evening.

     I've got something my mind.

d   Has Mrs Chen changed mind? I thought she was

     staying at the Hilton.

e   We're early. Let's go and have a coffee. It will keep

     your mind your driving test.

f   Although I'd met Vladimir several times before, my

     mind blank and I couldn't remember his name.

g   You've lost my pen? Oh, mind. It wasn't valuable.

h   Would you mind me with my suitcases?

i   Dave is so minded. He got all the way to the theatre

     and then realised he'd got the wrong date.

j   I made my mind not to take the job.

k   Mind gap between the train and the platform.

l   Bearing mind the fact that we've only had a week, I

     think we've produced a very good plan.

m   Celebrities shouldn't complain if people take photos

     of them, my mind.

n   Yes, I got a pay rise, but no, I'm not going to tell you

     how much. Mind your business!

o   My new secretary is surprisingly honest. She

     certainly her mind.

MODULE 5

Vocabulary
Remarkable achievements

1 Complete the gaps with words or phrases from page 52 of the Students' Book.

Heroes
....

Mother Teresa of Calcutta (a) p r o v i d e s   a n important r o l e   m o d e l for twenty-five percent of young Italians, according to a recent survey. The nun, who spent all her life helping the poor in Calcutta and (b) r _ _ _ _ _ g large s _ _ _ of money for them, came top in the survey ahead of the Pope. People voted for them because of their (c) d _ d _ _ _ _ _ _ to the work of helping others and their incredible (d) s _ _ _ _ _ a.

Sixty-four-year-old Ian Cameron was shot yesterday when he chased after two robbers he saw running from a bank. 'I felt no (e) s _ _ _ _ of d _ _ _ _ _ at the time,' he said later. 'I just did what I thought was right.' 'He is a brave man but he (f) t _ _ _ a huge r _ _ _,' said Detective Inspector Sally Carter. 'He could have been killed.'

Frida Kahlo, the (g) e x _ _ _ _ _ _ _ _ _ _ _ t _ _ _ _ _ _ d Mexican artist, was seriously hurt in a bus accident at the age of eighteen and suffered damage to her spine, shoulder, leg and foot. She had more than thirty operations, but still (h) s _ _ _ _ _ _ _ severe p h _ _ _ _ _ _ pain for the rest of her life. In spite of having to (i) c _ _ _ w _ _ _ these problems, Kahlo enjoyed life to the full. She died in 1954 at the age of forty-seven.

Oprah Winfrey has been named one of the 100 Most Influential People of the Twentieth Century for her work as a campaigner for women's and children's rights and promoter of reading. She (j) o v _ _ _ _ _ _ a difficult early life and a background of abuse to become an actor and later a talk show host and presenter of the *Oprah Book Club*. Through her various projects, she has (k) m _ _ _ a f _ _ _ _ _ _, becoming the first African American woman millionaire.

Future perfect or simple

2 Choose the correct alternative.

a   I can't wait until July! I won't *have* / have had a break since Christmas, so I'll really *need* / *have needed* a holiday.

b   My New Year's resolutions are to go on a diet and to stop smoking. This time next year I'll *lose* / *have lost* weight and I'll *have* / *have had* more money to spend.

c   A: Here's the film – will the photos *be* / *have been* ready by Thursday?
    B: Oh, I'm afraid we won't *do* / *have done* them by then – call in on Friday.

d   A: What's your decision on the takeover deal?
    B: Can you give me until tomorrow? By then I'll *have* / *have had* more time to think about it and I'll *give* / *have given* you my decision.

e   Maria is doing a two-week lecture tour in Russia – when she gets back she'll *visit* / *have visited* ten cities and I'm sure she'll *feel* / *have felt* absolutely exhausted!

Perfect tenses in the past, present and future

3 Match a sentence in column A with a response in column B. Complete each gap with the correct form of *have*.

A

1 Oh dear, I think I ____'ve____ broken your video.

2 You look slimmer than last time I saw you.

3 Shall I phone back at three?

4 How long _____ you had your car?

5 When _____ finished dinner?

6 You were in a bad mood yesterday.

7 _____ you seen Mrs Jones this morning?

8 Here are your glasses.

B

a Yes, I _____ slept well the night before.

b Oh, thank you, I thought I _____ lost them.

c Let's have a look.

d Thanks, I _____ lost 6 kilos.

e No, she won't be in till this afternoon.

f For about five years, and it's still very reliable.

g Mm, the meeting _____ finished by then. Try at four.

h Probably by about eight-thirty, so you could phone then.

Pronunciation
Contractions and weak forms

4 **a** **T5.1** Listen and repeat.

I've	I've lost	
I haven't	I haven't heard	
I'd	I'd lost them	
I hadn't	I hadn't slept	
You'll	You'll have /jləv/	You'll have done it
Won't	Won't have /wəntəv/	Won't have finished

b **T5.2** Look at exercise 3 again. Listen to the dialogues and try to read the answers in column B at the same time as the recording.

c **T5.3** Listen and repeat the questions.

Have you
/həvj/

Have you seen
Have you seen Mrs Jones?

How long
How long have
/halɒŋəv/

How long have you had ...?

Had you
/hədʒ/

Had you met ...?

d **T5.4** Listen and write the questions you hear.

1 *How long have you known her?* _____ (6 words)

2 _____ _____ _____? (7 words)

3 _____ _____ _____? (6 words)

4 _____ _____ _____? (8 words)

5 _____ _____ _____? (6 words)

6 _____ _____ _____? (5 words)

e Listen again and repeat the questions.

Vocabulary booster
Feelings

5 **a** Complete the sentences with the words and phrases from the box.

ashamed	disorientated	~~embarrassed~~	fed up
frustrated	grateful	guilty	inspired	left out
proud	unprepared	upset	

1 I felt terribly _embarrassed_ because she'd already told me her name three times and I'd forgotten it again!

2 Sam felt very _____ of his son when he won the award for best young journalist of the year.

3 She was very _____ when she heard that her grandfather had died.

4 I feel completely _____ for this exam. I haven't spent any time revising.

5 I'm feeling really _____ because I haven't phoned my mother for a month.

6 Tom felt really _____ after he'd done the creative writing course. He just wanted to go out and write a book!

7 I'm _____ with the weather. It's been wet and cloudy every day for three weeks.

8 Sue felt very _____ because she'd phoned the manager five times and he still hadn't called her back.

9 Don was _____ of his behaviour the night before so he phoned Saul and apologised.

10 Jenny felt _____ because she hadn't been in the building before and it was all very confusing.

11 When I was young I often felt _____ because the other children didn't play with me.

12 I'm really _____ for all your help with the party. Thanks a lot.

b **T5.5** Listen and check. Then listen again and repeat the words.

Vocabulary
Verb–noun combinations

6 **a** Complete the gaps with words from the verb–noun combinations on page 56 of the Students' Book. Then choose the correct answer.

1 When he was very young, Charles Darwin _showed_ a great interest in:
   a chess   b football   c worms

2 Which canal _____ it possible in 1869 to travel from the Mediterranean Sea to the Red Sea?
   a the Suez Canal   b the Grand Canal
   c the Panama Canal

3 Who _____ a world record for the first Pacific hot-air balloon crossing?
   a Richard Branson and Per Lindstrand
   b Bertrand Piccard and Brian Jones
   c Steve Fossett

4 In his thirties, Beethoven had to _____ with:
   a losing his sight   b losing his voice
   c losing his hearing

5 Who won the _____ for Best Actor in the 2004 Oscars?
   a Johnny Depp   b Sean Penn   c Bill Murray

6 Bob Geldof has campaigned to _____ which issue with world leaders?
   a third world debt   b child employment
   c the destruction of the rain forests

7 Which team _____ Germany to win the Football World Cup in 2002?
   a Italy   b Brazil   c Argentina

b **T5.6** Listen and check.

c Complete these sentences so that they are true for you.

1 I have never beaten _____

_____ .

2 I once won a _____

_____ .

3 I find it difficult to cope with _____

_____ .

4 I once raised money for _____

5 I think I'm making progress in _____

_____ .

6 If I ever make a fortune, I'll _____

_____ .

Listen and read
Greatest superheroes of all time

7 a **T5.7** Listen to and/or read the article. Which of these superheroes are being described?

Batman   The Incredible Hulk   Spiderman   Superman   Wonder Woman
Xena, Warrior Princess   The X-men

Greatest Superheroes of All Time

With their simple stories of good versus evil, comic-book superheroes are as popular today as when they first appeared. So who are these much-loved characters?

Here is a brief introduction to four of the greatest superheroes of all.

1 _____

In 1939 America, DC Comics seized on the public's desire for escapism during a period of social and economic deprivation, and developed a new superhero. The creators of the 'Man of Steel' wanted a hero in a colourful costume who would look good in a comic book. Although there had been superheroes before, this was the first 'total package' with a costume, secret identity and abilities beyond those of mortal men. Born in a far-off galaxy, the baby hero discovers as he grows up that our sun gives him extraordinary powers: he can fly 'faster than a speeding bullet', has incredible strength and X-ray vision, and can only be hurt or destroyed by a green rock from his original planet, Krypton. He is adopted and brought up by Martha and Jonathan Kent to uphold truth, justice and the 'American way'. Whenever danger calls, he is never far from a telephone box and a quick change, ready to save the world. He's had several TV and film incarnations, the most successful of which starred Christopher Reeve and Margot Kidder in 1978. Ironically, creators Siegel and

Shuster signed away their rights to the character for $130!

2 _____

Born on Paradise Island, youthful and immortal, this princess has been blessed by ancient gods and goddesses with powers of super strength and speed and the ability to fly. The superheroine made her first appearance in 1941. It is said she was invented by William Marston for DC Comics as a role model for girls and to raise the morale of US troops in World War II. Her alter-ego, Diana Price, works as a hospital nurse, but transforms herself by flicking her lasso. As well as the lie-detecting lasso, she

has bracelets which can stop bullets, but unfortunately she loses her powers if she is tied up with her own lasso. She is instantly recognisable by her stars and stripes costume and in 1976 her adventures were brought to life in a three-year TV series starring ex-Miss USA Beauty Queen, Linda Carter.

3 _____

Created by artist Bob Kane and writer Bill Finger for DC Comics, the stories combined superheroics and a secret identity. This character cannot stop bullets, fly, or look through walls. He is a normal man who becomes one of the greatest crimefighters ever because of his detective skills, highly trained physical abilities, amazing gadgets, and of course, his 'batmobile' car, kept in a hidden cave beneath his mansion. By day he is rich socialite Bruce Wayne, but at night he turns into 'the caped crusader', accompanied by his side-kick, Robin. He was memorably brought to life in the 1960s TV series and in the film of 1996 starring Michael Keaton, Kim Basinger and Jack Nicholson – a film that featured four of the series' best arch-villains: Catwoman, The Joker, The Penguin and The Riddler.

4 _____

Like many other superheroes, Peter Parker is an orphan, although he has an uncle (Ben) and aunt (Mae). Part of his appeal is that both adolescents and adults can readily identify with him. A poor school student, he goes on to become a regular working guy: a high-school teacher with both girlfriend and money problems. His world is turned upside down when his Uncle Ben is murdered. He gains his superpowers during a high school science demonstration when a radiated spider bites him and gives him superhuman strength and reflexes and the ability to stick to most surfaces. In the movie, which was the biggest money spinner of 2002, Parker grows webslingers which shoot and spin webs, and puts on his red and blue costume to fight arch-enemies such as the Green Goblin and Doctor Octopus.

b Listen and/or read again and answer the questions.

1 How was Superman different from previous superheroes?

_____
_____
_____

2 Where do his powers come from?

_____

3 What is Superman's only weakness?

_____
_____

4 Who is Martha Kent?

_____

5 Who gave Wonder Woman her powers?

_____

6 Why was Wonder Woman created?

_____
_____

7 What is an 'alter-ego'?

_____

8 What three things can Wonder Woman's lasso do?

_____
_____

9 In what important way is Batman different from the other three superheroes?

_____
_____

10 Who is Batman's alter-ego?

_____

11 Who is his companion in crime-fighting?

_____

12 What happened to Peter Parker's parents?

_____

13 Was he born with his superpowers?

_____

14 What two things can he do which give him the name Spiderman?

_____
_____

Present perfect simple or continuous

8 Complete the gaps with the best form of the verb in brackets. Remember to use contractions.

A computer help line

a 'I _ve been working___ (work) all morning on a document and I _____ (only / manage) to print two pages of it.'

b 'I _____ (make) some back-up disks and I think I _____ (lose) one of my files.'

An English student

c 'I'm fed up. This is the third time I _____ (fail) the First Certificate Exam and I _____ (study) here for three years now.'

d 'I _____ (look) for an English–Polish dictionary in the library, but I _____ _____ (only / find) a 1965 edition. The librarian said I should talk to you.'

A radio phone-in programme about health

e 'I feel terrible. I _____ _____ (wake up) at 5 a.m. for the last month. I _____ _____ (try) two different kinds of sleeping pill, but they just make me feel worse.'

f 'My husband _____ (behave) strangely recently. He _____ (start) talking to himself and he _____ (stop) going out with his friends. What do you think's wrong with him?'

Improve your writing

Giving news in an e-mail

9 Use the prompts to write Alan's e-mail to his old friend Tom.

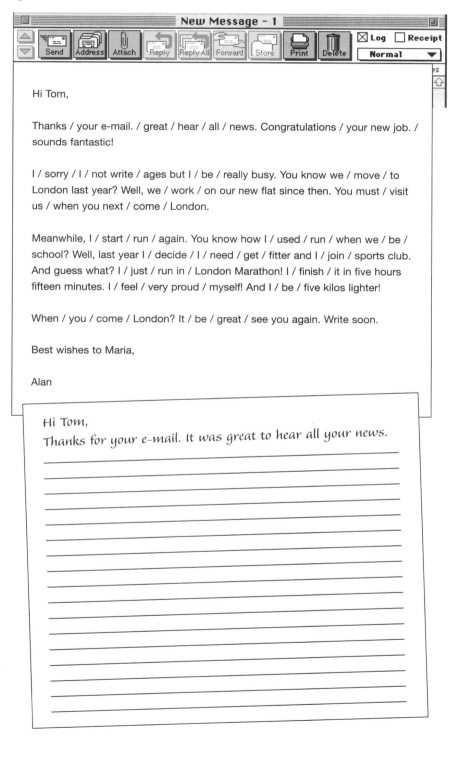

New Message - 1

Send Address Attach Reply Reply All Forward Store Print Delete

☒ Log ☐ Receipt

Normal ▼

Hi Tom,

Thanks / your e-mail. / great / hear / all / news. Congratulations / your new job. / sounds fantastic!

I / sorry / I / not write / ages but I / be / really busy. You know we / move / to London last year? Well, we / work / on our new flat since then. You must / visit us / when you next / come / London.

Meanwhile, I / start / run / again. You know how I / used / run / when we / be / school? Well, last year I / decide / I / need / get / fitter and I / join / sports club. And guess what? I / just / run in / London Marathon! I / finish / it in five hours fifteen minutes. I / feel / very proud / myself! And I / be / five kilos lighter!

When / you / come / London? It / be / great / see you again. Write soon.

Best wishes to Maria,

Alan

Hi Tom,
Thanks for your e-mail. It was great to hear all your news.

_____

_____

_____

_____

_____

_____

_____

_____

_____

_____

_____

_____

_____

_____

Wordspot
first

10 Replace the words in bold with a phrase with *first* from page 60 of the Students' Book.

a   We travelled **in the best seats**.

   first-class   (2 words)

b   **Initially** I found the job very difficult.

   _____ (2 words)

c   They fell in love **when they first saw each other**.

   _____ (3 words)

d   The truck went up the hill **in its lowest gear**.

   _____ (3 words)

e   Carmen's **mother tongue** is Spanish.

   _____ (2 words)

f   I did a course in **giving simple medical help**.

   _____ (2 words)

g   **To start with** you need to stand with your skis parallel.

   _____ (3 words)

h   You can see Venus **very early** in the morning.

   _____ (2 words)

i   Patrick is **friendly enough** with the President **to use his Christian name**.

   _____ (4 words)

j   I'm afraid your **preferred** holiday dates are not available.

   _____ (2 words)

k   When I saw the apartment my **initial feelings** were very positive.

   _____ (2 words)

l   '... coming round the bend, Michael Schumacher is **leading**.'

   _____ (3 words)

Listen and read
How to …

1 a T6.1 Listen to and/or read the stories. Choose the best heading for each one.

How to invest money successfully	How to get the attention of the police
How to get a table at a restaurant	How to prevent a burglary
How to make money	How to reserve a table at a restaurant

A

How to _____

A young man asked a rich old man how he had become wealthy. The old man said, 'Well, son, it was 1932 in the depth of the Great Depression. I was down to my last cent. I invested that cent in a golf ball. I spent the day polishing the golf ball and at the end of the day I sold it for two cents. The next morning I invested that two cents in two golf balls. I spent the entire day polishing them and sold them for four cents. I continued like this for a few weeks and by the end of that time I'd accumulated a hundred dollars.

'Then my wife's father died and left us three million dollars.'

B

How to _____

Stewart Montgomery of Glasgow, Scotland was going to bed one night when his wife peered out of the bedroom window and told him he'd left the light on in the garage. Montgomery opened the back door to go and switch off the light but saw that there were two men moving about in the garage.

He phoned the police, who asked, 'Is there actually a burglar in your house?' When he said no, they told him to lock all his doors and stay inside; no one was free at the moment but someone would come when available. Montgomery hung up, waited a minute, and then phoned back.

'Hello. I just called to tell you that there were burglars in my garage. Well, you don't have to worry about them now because I've just shot them both.'

Within two minutes, four police cars and an ambulance screeched to a halt outside his house. At least ten police officers rushed into the garage and caught the men red-handed. One of the policemen said to Stewart, 'I thought you said you'd shot them!' 'I thought you said there was no one available!' replied Montgomery.

C

How to _____

A couple went into an exclusive restaurant in Los Angeles. 'I'm sorry,' said the head waiter, 'but there are no tables available.'

'Do you know who I am?' said the man. 'I am Dwayne Wright, the film director.'

'I'd like to help you, Mr Wright, but there are no tables left tonight.'

'I'm certain that if the President came in and asked for a table, there would be one free.'

'Well, I suppose so, … yes,' said the waiter after a brief pause. 'Yes, there would be a table for the President.'

'Good. I'll take it. The President isn't coming this evening, so I'll have his table!'

b Listen and/or read again. Who …

1 inherited something?
_____

2 was polite but firm?
_____

3 lied? _____

4 was hesitant? _____

5 was diligent and hardworking?
_____

6 was persuasive? _____

c Replace the words in bold with a word or phrase from the stories. The letter in brackets shows in which story you will find the word or phrase.

1 They were **very rich** and lived in a beautiful mansion. (A)
  *wealthy*_____

2 Things were pretty bad: I'd lost my job and my home, and I **hardly had any money left**. (A)
_____

3 Over the years, we've **steadily collected** an enormous number of books. (A)
_____

4 She **looked carefully** round the door, hoping he'd gone. (B)
_____

5 After I'd **put the phone down** I regretted being so rude to her. (B)
_____

6 He saw the red traffic light at the last minute and **stopped suddenly with a terrible noise**. (B)
_____

7 The police arrived at the bank and caught the robber **in the act of committing a crime**. (B)
_____

8 There was a **short silence** and then the audience broke into deafening applause. (C)
_____

d **T6.2** Listen and check.

Articles
a/an and *the* – first and second mention

2 Put five indefinite articles (*a/an*) and five definite articles (*the*) in the correct places in the joke.

> *An*
> ∧Old man was backing BMW into parking space when bright red sports car drove in behind him and took space. Young man jumped out and said, 'Sorry, old man, but you've got to be young and fast to do that.' Old man ignored young man and kept reversing until BMW had destroyed sports car completely. 'Sorry, son, you've got to be old and rich to do that!'

Making generalisations

3 Complete the pairs of sentences with a word from the box, then insert *the* where necessary.

exercise	poetry	~~traffic~~	music	people
men / women				

a 1 ___Traffic___ is one of the biggest problems in our cities.

  2 Sorry we're so late. _The traffic_ on the way here was really bad.

b 1 What a dreadful party! _____ all talked about their children and _____ all talked about sport!

  2 _____ are much better at multi-tasking than _____.

c 1 I was doing _____ you showed me for twenty minutes yesterday and it made my legs ache!

  2 _____ is really good for you.

d 1 I hate _____ who chew gum all the time.

  2 I thought _____ at the next table were very rude to the waiter.

e 1 Janet doesn't like listening to _____ when she works.

  2 _____ they play on Radio 5 is terrible.

f 1 _____ of Dante is very passionate.

  2 We studied _____ at school, but I haven't read much since.

the with places

4 Complete the gaps in the holiday advertisement with *the* where necessary.

Winter Breaks with Sunspot Holidays

Visit (a) ___ *Australia!*

* Spend the first three days in (b) _____ **Sydney**
* See (c) _____ **Sydney Harbour Bridge**
* Go shopping in (d) _____ **George Street**
* Visit (e) _____ **Blue Mountains**, just outside the city.
* Then go north to (f) _____ **Whitsunday Islands** and practise your diving in (g) _____ **Pacific Ocean.**
* Finally, see the crocodiles from the film *Crocodile Dundee* in (h) _____ **Kakadu National Park.**

This is a once in a lifetime offer! Fourteen days that you'll never forget.

* **Call 010 600 4000 now.**

a/an and *the* with institutions, e.g. *school*

5 Cross out *the* or *a* in the sentences below if they are unnecessary.

a 1 Nelson Mandela spent many years in the prison.
  2 The prison was a long way from June's house, so she couldn't visit her husband very often.
b 1 I cycle past the hospital every morning on my way to work.
  2 My sister has been in a hospital since her operation.
c 1 Billy's still at the school; his lessons don't finish until four o'clock.
  2 Elena works at the local school as a teaching assistant.
d 1 I waited in the church for the rain to stop.
  2 We go to the church every Sunday for the ten-thirty service.
e 1 I left the university when I was twenty-one.
  2 My parents only visited the university once, on my graduation day.

6 Complete the gaps in the extracts with *a*, *an*, *the* or no article (–).

Flying problems

Nearly all (a) _____–_____ air travellers suffer from (b) _____ jet lag to some extent. In (c) _____ recent survey, only five percent said they had never had (d) _____ problem. (e) _____ most common complaints were (f) _____ tiredness and (g) _____ disturbed sleep for up to five days after flying.

Here are some tips to help:
* try to book (h) _____ morning flight;
* avoid (i) _____ alcohol and drink plenty of (j) _____ still water;
* get up and walk around (k) _____ plane regularly;
* when you get to your destination, try not to sleep during (l) _____ next day and go outside as much as possible.

Depression

(m) _____ Canadian study may help to explain why (n) _____ women are more likely to suffer from (o) _____ depression and (p) _____ eating problems than (q) _____ men. (r) _____ Canadian study shows that (s) _____ women's brains produce around 37 percent less serotonin, (t) _____ important factor in many key brain functions, including (u) _____ regulation of (v) _____ mood and appetite.

7 Read these tips from a magazine about finding a good fitness club.
Six of the lines are correct and seven have an unnecessary article.
Tick (✓) the correct lines. Circle the unnecessary articles (*a/an/the*).

1	(The) many people go to a gym regularly, to try to
2	lose the weight and cope with the stress of modern life.
3	Here are the some tips for finding the best gym for you.
4	Visit at least three clubs at the time of day you plan to work out.
5	Check for the cleanliness, especially in the changing rooms.
6	Ensure the equipment is well maintained and suited to your
7	requirements. Expect the well-qualified, presentable instructors.
8	Check that an instructor is available in the gym area at all times
9	for an assistance. Is the club security-conscious – do you need
10	an ID card to get in? Do you need to pay a membership fee and
11	does the fee include the cost of aerobics classes? Choose a gym
12	a short distance away – if it takes you more than the thirty minutes
13	to get there, you probably won't go.

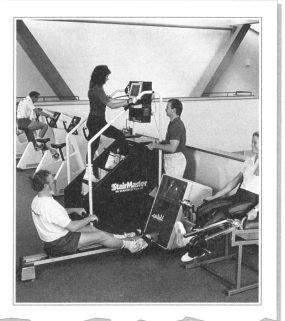

8 Use the prompts to write full sentences, paying attention to the use of articles.

a At / Christmas / my mother usually / go / to / church at eight o'clock, then she / come / home and / cook / huge lunch.

_____

_____

_____

b Deborah / leave / home / last year – now she / work / as / lecturer in / Vancouver.

_____

_____

c I / visit / Uncle Frank in / hospital / yesterday morning. He / be / very lucky, because he / have / got one of / best heart specialists in / UK.

_____

_____

_____

d A: Be / Jamie happy at / school?
   B: Yes. He / like / teachers, and / school / be only / five minutes away, in / Kilmorie Road.

_____

_____

_____

e Gordon / be / terrible cook. He / invite / us for / dinner / last Saturday evening and it / be / one of / worst meals / I / ever / have.

_____

_____

_____

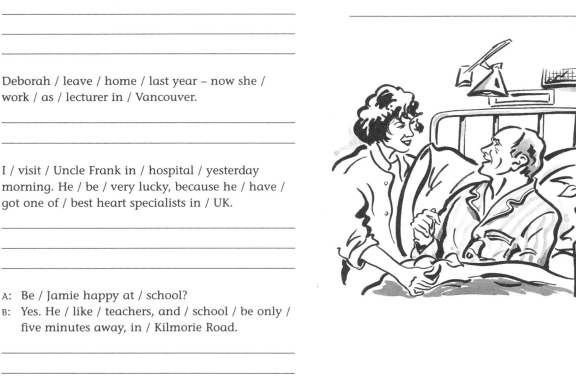

Different ways of giving emphasis

9 **a** Make this soap opera script more dramatic by adding the words from the box in a suitable place. The words are in the correct order.

~~so~~   on earth   completely   far too   really do   absolutely   far too absolutely

---

Drew enters the flat, to see Jenny looking very upset. The noise of plates smashing and screaming can be heard coming from the kitchen.

JENNY: Oh Drew, I'm *so* pleased to see you …

DREW: Why? What's all that shouting in the kitchen?

JENNY: It's Simon – he's gone mad, because he thinks
Anna's seeing someone else.

DREW: (*walking towards the kitchen*) Right, I'm going to
stop this …

JENNY: (*running after him and pulling him back*) No, it's
dangerous! He's got a knife!

DREW: You don't think he'll use it, do you?

JENNY: I think he might, because he's been drinking …
Anna's terrified.

DREW: (*walking around agitatedly*) This is ridiculous …
let's try and talk to him.

JENNY: It won't do any good, he's drunk.

DREW: (*picking up the phone*) Okay then, let's call the
police – there's nothing else we can do.

Anna and Simon

Jenny and Drew

b **T6.3** Listen to some extracts from the dialogue and mark the words which carry the main stress on the script above.

c Listen again and repeat.

Cleft sentences

Remember how we can change the word order to emphasise a certain part of a sentence:

- *Her terrible accent annoyed me most.*
- ***What annoyed me most was** her terrible accent.*

- *Mike left all the windows open.*
- ***It was Mike who** left all the windows open.*

10 **a** Rearrange the words to make cleft sentences. The first word is underlined.

1 grandmother – gave – was – who – awful – It – that – my – me – picture

   It was my grandmother who gave me that awful picture.

2 like – hot – What – a – bath – feel – is – nice – I – really

   _____

   _____

3 It – crashed – me – car – who – the – wasn't

   _____

   _____

4 designs – I've – are – latest – got – our – What – here

   _____

   _____

5 who – play – through – It – slept – the – was – all – you

   _____

   _____

6 who – was – 1998 – It – won – World Cup – France – the – in

   _____

   _____

7 about – impressed – was – enthusiasm – me – his – What – Sam

   _____

   _____

b Change these sentences to give more emphasis, using *What* and *It*.

1 I hate living here because of the pollution.
   What I hate about living here is the pollution.

2 I love autumn because of the colour of the leaves.
   What _____ .

3 John didn't pay for the wedding ring, Sarah did.
   It _____ .

4 You need a new car.
   What _____ .

5 Did you choose the furniture?
   Was _____ .

6 I don't understand how my sister paid for three holidays this year.
   What _____ .

Pronunciation
Cleft sentences

In this type of sentence, we often stress the verb in the *What* clause.

- *What I **like** about Madrid is the **nightlife**.*
- *What I **hate** about cooking is the **washing-up**.*
- *What **annoys** me about him is his **laziness**.*
- *What **interests** me most about languages is how **different** they are.*

11 **a** Listen to the sentences above and repeat, paying attention to the rhythm.

b Complete these sentences so that they are true for you, then practise saying them with the correct rhythm.

1 What I like about _____ is _____

   _____ .

2 What I hate about _____ is _____

   _____ .

3 What annoys me about _____ is _____

   _____ .

4 What interests me most about _____ is _____

   _____

   _____ .

So and *such*

12 **a** Here are some complaints about holidays. Decide if they are about a hotel (H), a train station (S), or a day-trip (DT).

1   I've never had such awful food, or known such rude waiters.

    __H__

2   The announcements were so unclear – we had no idea which platform to go to.

    _____

3   We had so little time to look around that it wasn't worth getting off the bus. It was such a waste of money.

    _____

4   It was such a long way from the sea, we had to get a bus.

    _____

5   There were so many people that I couldn't get on the train.

    _____

b Put *so*, *such* or *such a* in front of these words and phrases.

__so__ expensive   _____ mess

_____ much traffic   _____ loud music

_____ friendly tour guide   _____ comfortable beds

c Complete the sentences with a word or phrase from the box, and add *so*, *such*, *such a*, *so many* or *so much*.

information ~~bad~~ good time times crowded terrible weather

1   The traffic was _____so bad_____ that we missed our flight.

2   We don't usually have _____ at this time of year.

3   Everyone had _____ at the barbecue.

4   They didn't expect the exhibition to be _____ .

5   Janet's seen the film _____ that she knows every line.

6   There was _____ in the report that I didn't have time to read it.

Improve your writing
Taking notes: abbreviations

13 **a** Find an abbreviation in the box for each of the words and phrases below.

re. a.m. Sat. N.B. i.e. p.m. a.s.a.p. inc. etc. ~~e.g.~~ P.S. &

1   __e.g.__ for example

2   _____ as soon as possible

3   _____ and

4   _____ et cetera

5   _____ Saturday

6   _____ this means / which means

7   _____ please note

8   _____ about

9   _____ morning

10   _____ afternoon

11   _____ including

12   _____ postscript (a message written at the end of a letter, after the signature)

b Complete the sentences with an abbreviation.

1   You can put different toppings on your pizza, __e.g.__ cheese, tomato, olives or ham.

2   I had to get up at 6 _____ to catch the train.

3   We went to all the famous places – Times Square, Broadway, Central Park, _____ .

4   Fish _____ chips: €6.50.

5   Mrs Lawrence phoned. Please ring back _____ .

6   The coach leaves on _____ at 9.30. You'll need to bring a packed lunch.

7   Mary – please phone your dentist _____ your appointment.

8   The film is only open to adults, _____ people over eighteen.

9   The CDs cost $40, _____ post and packaging.

10   That's all for now, see you soon,

    John

    _____ I love you!

Writing notes

When we write notes (such as phone messages) we miss out obvious words and use dashes (–) and abbreviations:

- *Your mum rang at 11.30. She's still expecting you this weekend. She's out on Saturday morning from 9 to 11 and she'll leave the key with Mrs Benson next door.*
- *11.30 – your mum rang – still expecting you this weekend. Out Sat a.m. 9–11 – will leave key with Mrs Benson next door.*

We miss out:
- pronouns (*he, she, it,* etc.)
- auxiliary verbs (*'s,* etc.)
- verb *to be* (*'s*)
- prepositions (*on, in, at,* etc.)
- articles (*the, a/an*)

14 Change these full messages into shorter notes. Try to use approximately the number of words in the brackets. A contraction = 2 words, an abbreviation or time = 1 word.

a   Paul phoned at 6.00. He wants to know if you're coming to Anne's party on Saturday. Please ring him back as soon as possible.

   6.00 — Paul phoned. Wants to know if ...

_____

(about 15 words)

b   Mr Larsen phoned at 10.30. His plane is arriving at 9 o'clock, not 8 o'clock on Thursday morning.

_____

_____

(about 11 words)

c   I've gone to the gym. Autoclinic phoned about the car. It will be ready tomorrow afternoon.

_____

_____

(about 12 words)

d   Susie phoned at 3.00. She's going to see *Godzilla* tonight with Paul. They'll meet you in Shades wine bar at 7.00.

_____

_____

(about 15 words)

Real life
Giving advice and making suggestions

15   **a**   Match the sentences in column A with the responses in column B. Then complete the responses with phrases from page 70 of the Students' Book.

A

1   [d]   Grant can't decide what to do when he leaves school.

2   [ ]   My car insurance has gone up fifty percent. It's ridiculous!

3   [ ]   This television hasn't worked properly ever since I bought it.

4   [ ]   Is that the doctor? Thank goodness! My sister has just cut her hand on a knife and it's bleeding badly.

5   [ ]   And now Joey wants me to lend him $250.

6   [ ]   I never know what to have in Indian restaurants.

7   [ ]   I'd like to take the whole class to the Science Museum but it's quite expensive.

B

a   All right. The _____ _____ thing is _____ put pressure on the hand and raise it above her head.

b   If you _____ me, you _____ _____ a good chicken tikka.

c   I _____ take it back, if _____ _____ you.

d   _Has_ he _thought_ of _____ a sports instructor? He's good at most sports.

e   You _____ _____ try _____ for a group discount.

f   _____ my _____ . Don't lend him a cent!

g   How _____ _____ on the Internet? You can find some really good deals there.

b   [T6.5]   Listen and check. Repeat the advice or suggestion.

Vocabulary
Events and celebrations

1 Use the clues to find words from the box on page 72 of the Students' Book in the word square.

J	C	C	V	A	U	D	I	E	N	C	E	P
F	L	V	M	R	F	E	P	P	T	T	Y	L
F	A	N	C	Y	R	M	Q	Q	A	C	W	A
G	P	Y	B	C	R	O	W	D	B	A	S	C
O	S	K	K	L	Y	N	S	Q	T	R	W	A
K	P	R	O	C	E	S	S	I	O	N	B	R
Q	E	L	Z	P	L	T	Z	D	W	I	L	D
E	C	H	A	N	T	R	C	W	P	V	Q	T
W	T	B	A	W	B	A	B	A	U	A	K	C
S	A	M	F	Q	E	T	L	V	R	L	L	H
Z	T	R	L	S	I	I	N	E	Q	M	C	E
R	O	Y	A	D	C	O	N	C	E	R	T	E
T	R	L	G	F	R	N	B	A	N	N	E	R

a You do this by hitting your hands together continuously. _clap_

b If you are in the a_____ you are watching and listening to a public performance.

c You wear f_____ dress to look like a famous person or fictional character.

d People join a d_____ if they want to protest publicly about something.

e A c_____ is a large group of people in a public place.

f A p_____ is a line of people or vehicles moving slowly for an event.

g You do this by repeating a word or phrase rhythmically. c_____

h An outdoor c_____ is a musical event held in the open air.

i You are a s_____ if you are watching an event or a game.

j Each country has its own f_____ with a coloured pattern or picture on it.

k You do this by moving your hand or arm from side to side. w_____

l If people go w_____ , they behave in a very excited way.

m At a c_____ , there is dancing, drinking and a procession through the streets.

n A p_____ is a large notice which is posted or carried in a public place.

o You do this by shouting to show your approval or support. c_____

p A b_____ is a long piece of material with something written on it, often carried between two poles.

Vocabulary
Extreme adjectives

2 Replace the words in bold with an extreme adjective from page 73 of the Students' Book.

furious
There were (a) **very angry** scenes in Parliament today when the government's transport plans came under attack. 'It's (b) **very frightening** to think that the government is so out of touch with the country,' said the shadow Transport Minister.

(c) **Very big** crowds braved (d) **very cold** temperatures last night to see a rare open-air performance by the Three Tenors. After nearly an hour's delay, the singers came on to (e) **very noisy** applause.

Dear all,
arrived here (f) **very tired** after two-day drive through France. Staying in (g) **very small** village with (h) **very beautiful** views across the mountains. Weather (i) **very bad** so far, got (j) **very wet** on a boat on the lake today, but hoping that …

3 **a** Four of the sentences below are wrong. Correct the mistakes by changing the word in bold.

1 Wear a coat when you go out – it's **quite** cold for this time of year. ___✓___
2 I find the idea of bungee jumping **absolutely** frightening. _____
3 Catherine was **very** furious about the mess that the children had made. _____
4 Can you turn your music down, please? It's very **noisy**. _____
5 We've been moving house all day – we're absolutely **exhausted**. _____
6 Mum, I'm absolutely **hungry** – can I have a burger? _____
7 Have you seen the new sitcom on ABC? It's **really** funny. _____
8 Didn't you take an umbrella? You must be absolutely **wet**. _____

b **T7.1** Listen and check. Then listen and repeat, paying attention to the stressed words.

Pronunciation
Stress in extreme adjectives

4 **a** Put the extreme adjectives from the box under the correct stress pattern.

~~tiny~~ gorgeous furious fascinating starving huge freezing terrible terrifying soaked deafening hilarious spectacular exhausted amazing

1 ●	2 ●●	3 ●●●
	tiny	
4 ●●●●	**5 ●●●**	**6 ●●●●**

b **T7.2** Listen and check. Repeat the adjectives.

c **T7.3** Listen to the questions, and answer using an extreme adjective.

You hear:

Is it cold outside?

You say:

Yes, it's freezing.

Defining relative clauses

5 **a** Look at the statements from a survey on 'pet hates'. Match a sentence beginning in A with an ending in B.

A
1 I get really annoyed by cyclists
2 I hate people
3 I hate jeans
4 I really don't like parties
5 I can't stand the taste of cola
6 I hate days
7 I really don't like restaurants
8 I get annoyed by children
9 I hate sandwiches
10 I hate politicians

B
a where I don't know anyone.
b whose policies change as soon as they get into power.
c whose parents let them make a lot of noise.
d where the service is slow.
e that are too tight.
f that have too much butter in them.
g who talk loudly on their mobile phones on the train.
h which has gone flat.
i when I don't get anything finished.
j who ride on the pavement.

b **T7.4** Listen and check.

c Tick the sentences you agree with. Then write five sentences about your own pet hates, using *who*, *which*, *whose*, *when* and *where*.

1 I hate _____ .
2 I don't like _____ .
3 I can't stand _____ .
4 I really don't like _____ .
5 I get annoyed by _____ .

Non-defining relative clauses

6 **a** Read this summary of a short story called *The Model Millionaire* by Oscar Wilde.

Hughie Erskine, (1) <u>*who was a charming and attractive young man*</u> , was unfortunately not very successful in business and therefore did not have much money. He was in love with a beautiful girl called Laura Merton (2) _*who / that*_ _____ . One day Hughie went to visit his friend Alan Trevor (3) _____ . Trevor was just putting the finishing touches to a portrait of a beggar. The beggar (4) _____ looked sad and tired. 'Poor old man,' thought Hughie, 'he looks so miserable,' and gave the man a pound (5) _____ _____ . The beggar smiled and said, 'Thank you, sir, thank you.' Hughie spent the rest of the day with Laura (6) _____ _____ and he had to walk home because he had no money for a bus. The next day he went to a bar (7) _____ . Trevor told him that the 'beggar' was in reality Baron Hausberg (8) _____ _____ . Hughie felt deeply embarrassed about giving him the pound. The following day he received an envelope from the Baron (9) _____ _____ . The message on the envelope said: 'a wedding present to Hughie and Laura from an old beggar'.

b Add this extra information in the gaps in the story, using non-defining relative clauses. Include commas where necessary.

- she was annoyed because he had given away his last pound
- his financial skills had made him a millionaire
- he was an artist
- ~~he was a charming and attractive young man~~
- it was all the money he had
- her father had demanded £10,000 to allow them to marry
- he was wearing torn, shabby old clothes and holding out his hat for money
- it had a cheque for £10,000 inside it
- he met Alan Trevor there

c 〔 T7.5 〕 Listen and check.

7 In these extracts from an entertainment guide, join the sentences to make two longer ones, using relative pronouns.

CINEMA

Terminator 3 is the best of the *Terminator* series. It stars Arnold Schwarzenegger. This version is a 'must' for all Arnie fans. It includes new special effects.

a <u>*Terminator 3, which stars*</u> <u>*Arnold Schwarzenegger, is*</u> <u>*the best of the Terminator*</u> <u>*series. This version*</u> _____ _____

COMEDY

The Comedy Collection finishes on Friday. It features the brilliant Steve Jones and newcomer Martin Simons. Tickets are available on the door. They cost $12 and $16.

b <u>*The Comedy Collection*</u> _____ _____ _____

EXHIBITIONS

'Old New York' opens this weekend at the Brinkley Gallery. The Gallery has recently reopened. This exhibition of photographs takes you through fifty years of New York's history. It took six months to put together.

c <u>*'Old New York'*</u> _____ _____ _____ _____

Vocabulary booster
Describing food

8 **a** Match the adjectives in the box to the definitions.

> chewy   fattening   bland   juicy   crunchy   canned   pickled   spicy
> nourishing   crumbly   bitter   chilled   mouth-watering   poisonous
> ~~smoked~~   greasy

1   hung in smoke to give it a special taste __*smoked*__
2   breaks easily into small pieces _____
3   put in tins _____
4   has very little taste _____
5   can make you put on weight _____
6   needs to be chewed a lot before you can swallow it _____
7   looks or smells extremely good _____
8   covered in oil or fat _____
9   full of liquid _____
10   strong and healthy _____
11   very cold but not frozen _____
12   makes you very ill and can kill you _____
13   not sweet; like black coffee _____
14   makes a noise when you bite it _____
15   kept in vinegar or salt water _____
16   has a strong hot flavour _____

b **T7.6** Listen and check. Then listen again and repeat.

c Which adjectives describe …

1   the taste of food? _____
2   the texture of food? _____
3   ways of treating food? _____
4   the effect food has on you? _____

d Answer the questions.

1   Which of these is not usually smoked? *cheese, salmon, bread, ham*
2   Write the names of two foods which can be poisonous
_____
3   Which of these should not be chewy? *a toffee, a steak*
4   Write the names of two foods which are nourishing but fattening
_____
5   Which of these are not usually pickled? *onions, potatoes, beetroot*
6   Which of these is not crunchy? *a biscuit, an apple, a banana*

Wordspot
take

9 Replace the words in bold with a phrase with *take* from page 82 of the Students' Book.

a   You should *take off* **remove** all your jewellery before you go on a sunbed. (2 words)

b   How long **is the journey** to get to the station? (3 words)

c   Mrs Evans has offered to **look after** the cats while we're away. (3 words)

d   I noticed that you **wrote information down** during the presentation. (2 words)

e   I hope Stella didn't **consider my comments in a serious way** – I was only joking. (3 words)

f   Could you ask Mr Phelps to **sit down** and tell him I'll be with him in a minute. (3 words)

g   I don't think **I'm like** anyone in my family. (3 words)

h   Did you **photograph** the sunset? It looked amazing. (4 words)

i   Police reports say the accident **happened** just before midnight. (2 words)

j   My sister's spent a lot of money on equipment since she **started** photography. (2 words)

k   It's all right, Mrs Wilkins, **don't hurry** and tell us exactly what you saw. (3 words)

Listen and read
Did you know?

10 a **17.7** Listen to and/or read the extracts and match them to the questions below.

1 Why do onions make us cry? _____

2 When was chewing gum invented? _____

3 Why is it called a 'hamburger' when there is no ham in it? _____

4 Who discovered tea? _____

5 Why do doughnuts have holes? _____

A

The answer is really quite simple: because they come from Hamburg, in Germany. However, their history is more complicated than that, and the question of who actually invented the first hamburger remains a mystery. Some say it was a group of nomadic people called the Tartars who tenderised their beef by placing it under a horse's saddle, flattening it into a patty. Others believe it was the German immigrants who travelled to the United States during the 19th century, bringing with them their favourite meal called Hamburg Style Beef – a chopped, raw piece of beef. Some argue that Americans placed the first cooked beef patty on a roll at the St Louis World Fair in 1921.

B

This issue has been raised by dozens of bakers over the years, but most agree that the answer to this sticky question lies in the fact that the interior of these fried cakes would not cook fully without a hole in the centre.

Another theory holds that a sea captain named Hanson Gregory, while standing on deck one stormy night, found it impossible both to steer his vessel and eat his doughnut. Out of sheer frustration, he impaled it over one of the spokes of the ship's wheel, thereby creating a finger hold with which to grip the cake. Quite pleased with his ingenuity, Mr Gregory ordered the ship's cook to put holes in doughnuts from that day onwards.

Whatever the reason for the hole, the doughnut has been incorporated into the diets of people throughout the world for centuries. In fact, archaeologists found petrified doughnuts amongst the artefacts of a primitive Indian tribe.

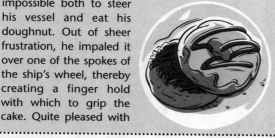

C

t is not the strong smell that makes us cry, but the gas that the onions release when we cut them. When this gas meets the water in our eyes, it produces sulphuric acid, which irritates our noses and eyes. One good tip, therefore, is to use a sharp knife, as this will crush the onion less and reduce the amount of gas released. Another good idea is to cut the root of the onion last or not at all, since this part produces the highest levels of the offending gas. Other less logical-sounding suggestions, which many people swear by, include putting the onion in the freezer for twenty minutes beforehand, having a bowl of water or a burning candle alongside while you chop, or putting a piece of bread in your mouth. The less self-conscious among us even keep a pair of swimming goggles handy for onion-chopping!

D

No one can be absolutely certain who the first gum chewers were, but historians tell us that civilisations around the world were chewing natural gum thousands of years ago. Before the invention of the electric light bulb or the telephone, people discovered the pleasure of chewing gum. The Mayans, an Indian civilisation that inhabited Central America during the second century, enjoyed chewing chicle, a natural gum from the sapodilla tree.

The American Indians introduced the custom of chewing gum (resin from the bark of spruce trees) to the early North American settlers, and these New Englanders created the first commercial chewing gum by selling lumps of spruce. Modern chewing gum appeared in 1869, when a Mexican general hired inventor Thomas Adams to develop a new form of rubber using chicle. Adams didn't manage to develop rubber, but he did succeed in producing the first modern chewing gum, which he called Adams New York No. 1.

E

Ancient folklore places the creation of the brew at 2737 BC. Shen Nung, an early emperor of China, was a skilled ruler, creative scientist and patron of the arts. His far-sighted edicts required, among other things, that all drinking water be boiled as a hygienic precaution.

One summer day while visiting a distant region of his realm, he and the court stopped to rest. In accordance with his ruling, the servants began to boil water for the court to drink. Blossom from a nearby camellia bush drifted into the boiling water and infused, producing a pale brown liquid. As a scientist, the Emperor was interested in the new liquid, drank some, and found it very refreshing. And so, according to legend, tea was created.

b Listen and/or read again. Complete the sentences, using information from the extracts.

1 Shen Nung's servants ___*boiled*___ water to make it safe to ___*drink*___ .

2 People were chewing gum before they had electric _____ or _____ .

3 The Tartars put their _____ under a horse's saddle to make it _____ .

4 If you use a _____ _____ to cut an onion, it will release less _____ .

5 Mr Gregory used the ship's _____ to make a _____ in his doughnut.

6 Some people believe that to prevent an onion from making you _____ , you should first put it in the _____ .

7 Legend says that _____ was first produced from _____ flowers.

8 Some people say that _____ were first served on _____ in America in 1921.

9 People all over the _____ have been eating doughnuts for _____ of years.

10 Modern chewing gum is made from the same natural gum that the _____ people used to chew in the _____ century.

Quantifiers

11 Correct the mistake in each sentence by crossing out or adding one word.

a Has everyone got enough ~~of~~ food?

b We know quite few of our neighbours, but not all of them.

c We had a lot fun learning to scuba dive today.

d I think we'll have a plenty of glasses for everyone.

e There are a number reasons why the President resigned.

f There was too much of food for four people to eat.

g Over fifty people applied for the job, but a very few of them had the right qualifications.

h There's a little of space for an extra chair here.

i There are only a few of places where you can buy this type of cheese.

j As any a doctor will tell you, you should eat a balanced diet.

12 Complete the gaps with quantifiers from the boxes below.

Rollerblades

The best: ☆☆☆☆☆ *Racers*

Super-fast and smooth, these skates come in (a) ___*a number of*___ different colours and have (b) _____ extra features, including holes which give (c) _____ of ventilation. One small reservation is that there's (d) _____ noise when you go at high speed.

The worst: ☆ *Grippers*

These skates take (e) _____ time to put on – almost 10 minutes and don't provide (f) _____ support for your feet. They come in (g) _____ colours – only grey, black or white.

enough plenty too much
quite a few very few
~~a number of~~ a great deal of

Choc 'n' Nut Ice cream

The best: ☆☆☆☆☆ *Naughty and Nutty*

This ice cream is full of flavour and should satisfy (a) _____ of the chocolate lovers among our readers. There are (b) _____ nuts and not (c) _____ sugar.

The worst: ☆ *Nut and Choc*

There are (d) _____ nuts in this ice cream, but not many, and (e) _____ chocolate. There is also (f) _____ sugar. A real disappointment.

too much (x2) any plenty of
some very little

CD Players

The best: ☆☆☆☆ *Genesis*

We tried (a) _____ CDs from pop to classical and (b) _____ kind of music sounded superb. There are only (c) _____ special features, but these are worthwhile and simple to use. The only problem is that (d) _____ shops actually have it in stock.

The worst: ☆ *Horizon*

We didn't think (e) _____ of the CDs played well. It looks quite futuristic but there are (f) _____ buttons and flashing lights for our liking.

any (x2) a number of
too many a few very few

Improve your writing
Describing a traditional dish

13 **a** Match the verbs to the pictures.

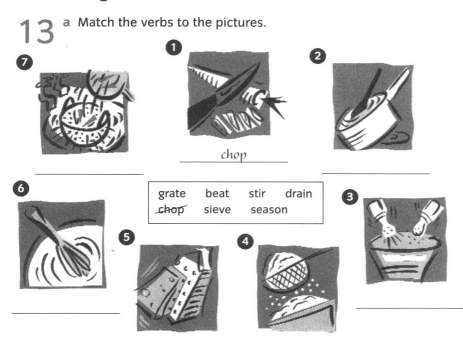

chop

grate   beat   stir   drain
chop   sieve   season

b Here are the lines of an e-mail that Marco sent his teacher, Frances. Write the text in the correct order.

New Message - 1

Send Address Attach Reply Reply All Forward Store Print Delete

☒ Log ☐ Receipt

Normal ▼

Dear Frances,

(A) As soon as it comes to the boil, put the spaghetti in, but **don't** turn the heat down, **or the pasta won't** cook properly (I've often seen English people doing this).

(B) **The next thing to do is** boil lots of salted water in a pan.

(C) Serve it with a good red wine and enjoy!

(D) **You start by preparing** the sauce: cut the bacon into little pieces and brown them on a low heat.

(E) That's it for now. I hope to come back to school after my summer holidays – give my best wishes to any of my classmates who are still there.

(F) **First of all, you'll** need 2 eggs, 20g of smoked bacon (it must be smoked), 20–30g of Parmesan cheese and 100g of spaghetti.

(G) **Next,** grate the cheese as finely as possible and stir it into the egg yolks.

(H) **Then** separate the egg whites from the yolks and beat the yolks in a bowl – **you can add** some salt and pepper at this point, **if you want to.**

(I) However, **make sure you don't** cook it for more than 8 minutes, or it'll be ruined.

(J) Here's that recipe I promised you for spaghetti alla carbonara, the way we *really* make it in Italy – that means *no cream*!

(K) **Now you just** need to drain it and add the bacon and the egg mixture to it. **When you've done this,** you don't need to put it back on the heat, because the egg will cook itself.

Ciao, Marco

c Write a recipe of a traditional or a favourite dish from your country to send to an English-speaking friend. Try to use some of the phrases in bold in Marco's recipe.

Real life
Awkward social situations

14 Rearrange the words to make responses, then write them below situations 1–5.

a   doesn't – slightest – It – the – matter – in

b   possibly – more – couldn't – any – I – manage –

c   again – see – How – to – you – lovely

d   eat – I – afraid – prawns – can't – I'm

e   love – able to – but – I'd – think – to come – I – don't – be – I'll

1   Your great aunt invites you to a history lecture, which you are sure will be very boring.
    I'd love to come, but I don't
    think I'll be able to.

2   Your girlfriend's mother offers you another piece of cake, but you don't really like it.
    _____
    _____

3   At a dinner party the host offers you some prawns, but you are allergic to them.
    _____
    _____

4   A woman comes up to you in a supermarket and tells you that you were at school together, but you don't remember her.
    _____
    _____

5   Your friend is upset because her puppy chewed your bag while you were at her house having coffee.
    _____
    _____

MODULE 8

Vocabulary
The road to fame

1 a Match beginnings in A with endings in B to make phrases from page 86 of the Students' Book.

A		B	
1	an overnight	a	attention
2	make ends	b	eye
3	be hounded	c	break
4	go into	d	decline
5	a starring	e	experience
6	be a huge	f	sensation
7	a burning	g	noticed
8	constant media	h	comeback
9	live in a huge	i	mansion
10	gain	j	role
11	be in the public	k	hit
12	get your first big	l	ambition
13	make a	m	meet
14	get yourself	n	by the paparazzi

b Complete the sentences with a phrase from part a, making any necessary changes to the verbs.

1 My son has a _burning ambition_ to become a professional footballer and play for England.

2 JK Rowling tries to protect her daughter from the _____ that surrounds her and her books.

3 I don't mind doing the job for nothing, I just want to _____ some _____ .

4 Tina Turner _____ as a solo artist after separating from her husband and co-artist, Ike.

5 Brad Pitt _____ when he appeared for fourteen minutes in the film *Thelma and Louise*, then he had _____ in *Dark Side of the Sun*.

6 I'd love to _____ , but I wouldn't like to have to clean it!

7 The Spice Girls released their first single in July 1996 and became _____ ; by Christmas of that year they were major international stars.

8 Although it looked as if his career _____ after he left Take That, Robbie Williams' album *Life through a Lens* _____ , selling over 300,000 copies.

9 Although Mozart was a very famous composer, he died in poverty, unable to _____ .

10 'Be in the limelight' is similar in meaning to 'b_____' .

11 I don't know if it was their off-stage behaviour or their music that _____ the band _____ , but anyway, they're big stars now.

12 Princess Diana _____ constantly _____ , and some people said they were partly responsible for her death.

Pronunciation
The letter 'a'

LOOK!

Compare these sounds:
/æ/ b<u>a</u>ck, s<u>a</u>ng
/eɪ/ m<u>a</u>ke, t<u>a</u>le
/ə/ c<u>a</u>reer, inevit<u>a</u>ble

2 a **T8.1** Listen to the words in the box (or say them aloud) and complete the table.

able   acting   ambition   attempt   attention
capture   constant   cre<u>a</u>te   f<u>a</u>me   grab
legend<u>a</u>ry   m<u>a</u>nsion   medi<u>a</u>   ordin<u>a</u>ry
outr<u>a</u>geous   re<u>a</u>lity   sens<u>a</u>tion   spect<u>a</u>tor

1	/æ/	2	/eɪ/	3	/ə/
	back		make		career
			able		

b **T8.2** Listen and check. Repeat the words.

Infinitives

3 Complete the gaps with a verb from the box, with or without *to*, positive or negative.

> answer   be   believe   borrow   come   eat
> find   go   ~~land~~   offer   read   see   suggest
> tell   thank   think

a   The President's plane is expected _to land_ at 9.30 tonight.

b   Thank you for the advice about Jess. Your comments really made me _____ .

c   I passed Maria in the street today, but she pretended _____ me.

d   I thought it was a very difficult exam. How many questions did you manage _____ ?

e   I think I'll buy Tessa some flowers _____ her for helping with Kim's party.

f   I told Vikki what Kate said about the redundancies at work, but she refused _____ me.

g   I'll let you _____ the car as long as you promise _____ careful with it.

h   Is it really necessary _____ every page of the document? It'll take ages!

i   Are you hungry? Can I get you something _____ ?

j   I understand your problem, but I really don't know what _____ .

k   Roy's Café is fine, but wouldn't you rather _____ somewhere special for your birthday?

l   I've had a row with Todd's brother and now he's threatening _____ to our wedding.

m   Why don't you use the Internet _____ the information you need for your project?

n   It's not easy for me _____ you this, but we've decided _____ you the job.

Gerunds

4 Rewrite the sentences so that the meaning stays the same, using the word in bold.

a   I read this article and I didn't look up any words in my dictionary. **without**

I read _this article without looking up any words in my dictionary._

b   In the summer you shouldn't go out in the midday sun. **avoid**

In the _____

_____ .

c   Al said he didn't eat the rest of the chocolates. **deny**

Al _____

_____ .

d   I'm finding it less strange to drive an automatic car. **getting used**

I'm _____

_____ .

e   I lost weight because I did lots of exercise and counted calories. **by**

I lost _____

_____ .

f   Tickets sell out quickly, so it's useful to phone the box office to check first. **worth**

Tickets sell out _____

_____ .

g   I'm sorry, madam, it's difficult for me to find your details on the computer. **trouble**

I'm sorry, madam, _____

_____ .

h   If it's not a problem for you to wait, I can get you a table next to the window. **don't mind**

If _____

_____ .

i   Do you think that you might apply for the job in Madrid? **considering**

Are _____

_____ ?

j   One of the best things about the summer is that you can eat outside. **able**

One of the best things _____

_____ .

k   You're going to see all your old school friends tomorrow. Are you excited? **looking forward**

Are you _____

_____ ?

l   I feel sad because I don't have the beach opposite my apartment any more. **miss**

I _____

_____ .

Gerund or infinitive?

5 Choose the correct alternative.

The Prime Minister was asked today how he plans (a) *deal with* / (to deal with) / *dealing with* growing crime amongst teenagers. He believes that it is important (b) *create* / *to create* / *creating* more jobs and (c) *provide* / *to provide* / *providing* more opportunities for them (d) *get* / *to get* / *getting* work. At the same time he thinks that we should (e) *be sent* / *to be sent* / *be sending* young criminals to prison for longer. 'The Labour Government is tough on crime', is his party's slogan. Parents must continue (f) *play* / *to play* / *playing* a vital role in (g) *help* / *to help* / *helping* the government (h) *make* / *to make* / *making* our streets safer. The government is also considering (i) *introduce* / *to introduce* / *introducing* a curfew in some city centres (j) *stop* / *to stop* / *stopping* young people being out on the streets after 11 o'clock, when most serious crimes happen.

6 Complete the gaps with a verb from the box in the infinitive (with or without *to*) or gerund form.

cheat   ~~find~~   find out   get   leave (x2)   meet (x2)
play   spend   trust   try

Big Brother ruined my love life, says Nasty Nick

Big Brother celebrity Nick Bateman says it's now impossible for him (a) ___to find___ a girlfriend because of his image. Bateman, a contestant on the reality show in which ten people agree (b) _____ twelve weeks together in a house full of cameras, was dubbed 'Nasty Nick' after he was made (c) _____ the house for (d) _____ to influence the other contestants' eviction nominations.
Since (e) _____ the house, Bateman has earned good money by (f) _____ on his evil image but his reputation has made it difficult for women (g) _____ him.
'Before BB, I had no trouble (h) _____ women, but now they can't (i) _____ away fast enough,' he told *The People* magazine.
'It would be great (j) _____ a woman who can see beyond what happened all those years ago and take time (k) _____ who I really am.'
Bateman, who still receives hate mail, added,
'(l) _____ is wrong and I'm sorry I did it, but I thought I was just playing the game.'

Different gerund and infinitive forms

7 **a** Six of the sentences below are wrong. Find the mistakes and correct them.

1 I've often wondered what it would be like
   be locked
   to ~~lock~~ up in a house for twelve weeks with nine strangers.

2 We looked everywhere for Pat and Rachel in the park, but they were nowhere to see.

3 One thing I love about weekends is not waking up by an alarm clock.

4 Katrova's performance in her last few matches is worrying: she appears to lose her confidence.

5 Has Marsha gone already? I'd like to have the chance to thank her before she left.

6 We're going to leave early because Jim's worried about being held up on the way to the airport.

7 I don't want to worry you, but there's a huge black rain cloud over there and it seems to come towards us.

8 I expected you to have finished that hours ago: why is it taking so long?

b T8.3 Listen and check.

8 **a** What are the customs for giving tips in your country? How much money would you give to:

a waiter? _____

a hairdresser? _____

a taxi driver? _____

b Complete the sentences with the correct form (infinitive, with or without *to*, or in the passive, or gerund) of the verbs in brackets.

1 In France, it is always worth _____*carrying*_____ (carry) a few francs for tips to taxi drivers, and it is customary _____ (give) a couple of francs to the cinema usher who shows you to your seat.

2 In the United States, it is not uncommon to see people _____ (chase) out of a restaurant by waiters for failing _____ (leave) a tip.

3 Life gets tricky in Japan, where people are expected _____ (show) gratitude, rather than actually hand over money.

4 How much _____ (tip) and when have always been tricky questions for the British.

5 Attitudes to tipping seem _____ (change) a lot in Britain over the last twenty years.

6 And finally, what are visitors to the UK advised _____ (do)?

7 Should tips _____ (include) in the minimum wage?

8 Holidays in the Middle East, where tipping is expected by nearly everyone, can _____ (get) very expensive.

9 Travellers to Scandinavia, where the cost of living is high, may _____ (be) relieved to find that tipping is not expected.

10 The report also angered waiters, waitresses and hairdressers by _____ (suggest) that tips should _____ (include) in the minimum hourly rate.

c The sentences in part b have been removed from this article about tipping. Decide where the sentences go in the text. There is one sentence which you do not need to use.

Some handy tips about tipping

The low pay debate highlights the practice that varies widely

a   _7_
This was the question being fiercely debated when the Government and unions clashed over the Low Pay Commission's report this week. The report suggests a minimum wage of £3.60 an hour, disappointing unions, which are campaigning for £4.61.

b _____
This will particularly affect those who work in restaurants where a service charge is included in the bill.

c _____
These issues are all the more topical because millions of them will soon be setting off on summer holidays to countries where customs vary widely. Here are some general guidelines on what to do.

d _____
The advice I was given by an American friend was: 'If in doubt, leave a tip.' This is a general rule of thumb. At a bar, for example, staff will expect you to leave them the change.

e _____
However, French law requires that restaurants, cafés and hotel bills include the service charge, usually 10–15 percent, so a tip is not expected.

f _____
For the more penny-pinching traveller, try Yemen, the only country in the region without a strong tipping culture.

g _____
There can be a serious loss of face for the people involved, such as waiters, if you try to insist on giving them a tip.

h _____
Hairdressers and people who work in restaurants will probably think you are mad if you try to leave a tip.

i _____
The popular travel guide *The Lonely Planet* has these suggestions. You should tip 10–15 percent of the total bill in a restaurant and round up taxi fares to the nearest 50p.

Listen and read
Harry Potter's magician

9 **a** `T8.4` Listen to and/or read the text about JK Rowling and decide if the statements are true (T) or false (F).

1 JK Rowling always knew that the Harry Potter books would make her famous. _____

2 She has made about £70m since she started writing. _____

3 She used to try to convince herself that she was not famous.

_____

4 Rowling's attitude to fame is more positive than negative.

_____

5 She tries to keep her daughter out of the public eye. _____

6 Her writing has been compared unfavourably with the words of a Spice Girls song. _____

7 Actor Stephen Fry read a shortened version of *The Philosopher's Stone* on the radio.

_____

8 Some people think that her books have a bad influence on children.

_____

b Without looking back at the text, match the two halves of the phrases. Then listen and/or read again and check.

best-selling	powers
to dream up	premieres
magical	phenomenon
a single	time
a publishing	author
film	mother
full	threats
death	a story

Harry Potter's magician

'In my wildest fantasy I could not have imagined anything like this,' JK Rowling said of the frenzy that surrounded the release of her last book. Her magical tales of wizards and witchcraft have prompted the biggest publishing sensation of modern times.

Joanne Kathleen Rowling dreamed up the story of Harry Potter, the bespectacled orphan blessed with magical powers, on a delayed train to Manchester in 1990. It has been a high-speed journey. Less than fifteen years ago she was an unemployed single mother, scribbling away at her first Potter draft in an Edinburgh café, dreaming of the day she could take up writing full time. Now she is a publishing phenomenon, with the series selling over 100 million books, translated into 42 different languages around the world. In 2001 alone she is estimated to have made £70m.

However, the best-selling author had difficulty coming to terms with the fame that this success brought her. 'For a long time people would ask me, "What's it like to be famous?" and I would say "I'm not famous." Now this was patently untrue, but it was the only way I could cope with it, by being in so much denial that I was virtually blind at times. Fame does have nice aspects, but for me personally, the negative outweighs the positive. It's a very odd and isolating experience. I know some people crave it, but I find that very hard to understand. It puts a great strain on your relationships.' Most of Rowling's friends have been doorstepped and offered money for stories about her and she feels guilty about that. She is also fiercely protective of her daughter Jessica's privacy, never using her in publicity or taking her to film premieres. She rarely talks about her, although when asked in an interview why she bought her London house, she laughed and explained that 'my daughter was getting a bit too used to room service' in the hotel where they had been staying.

The author is also not without her critics. One derided her work as having merit 'scarcely higher than a Spice Girls lyric'. Her characters, he said, were 'one-dimensional' and her appeal a product of over-hyped marketing. Accusations of arrogance have also been levelled at her. She refused to allow the BBC to shorten her work – an unprecedented move which encouraged Radio 4 to broadcast actor Stephen Fry's eight-hour reading of *The Philosopher's Stone* at Christmas in 2000.

There is also a darker side to Potter mania. Some people are obsessed with the idea that her books are teaching children about evil, and a few even believe that Rowling is a witch. 'I found death threats to myself on the Internet,' she says. 'I came across a Potter-hater site where people were being advised, well, to shoot me, basically. It was not a nice thing to find. It is bizarre. But what can you do?'

Improve your writing
Linking ideas and arguments

10 **a** Complete the student's composition with suitable linking words, paying attention to the punctuation and grammatical construction of the sentences. Use as many different linking words as possible.

Genius can take many different forms, but tends to be most common in fields such as music, mathematics, poetry or art. Some geniuses emerge very young – Mozart started composing at the age of five; (1) __however__ , others are late developers – Einstein was apparently very slow at school! It is also interesting that there tend to be far more male geniuses than female ones – or perhaps they are just given more encouragement. So what would it be like to be a genius? Is this something that most people would really want?

Obviously, there are many advantages. To begin with, all those things that other people struggle with, such as passing important exams, would come very easily to you if you were a genius. (2) _____ most ordinary people spend hours studying and revising, you would be able to walk into exams and score top marks without even trying. Wouldn't that be wonderful!

(3) _____ , it would be clear what your talents were, and (4) _____ choosing a career, or direction in life, would probably be much easier than for most people. And (5) _____ you might behave in a strange way sometimes, people would always respect and admire you because of your abilities.

(6) _____ , there are also important disadvantages. Because being so talented might make you feel special, you might find it difficult to relate to other people and (7) _____ find life a bit lonely sometimes. (8) _____ , you might end up feeling very superior to the rest of the world, never learning to value and respect other people properly. And, (9) _____ being so brilliant in certain areas, you might not learn important practical skills that other people have to learn and might not (10) _____ develop into a well-balanced person. In fact, you could end up leading rather a sheltered life, cut off from the real world, and all its up and downs.

On the whole, I think …

b Underline six more linking words in the composition.

Wordspot
big and *great*

11 Complete the sentences with either *big* or *great* and a word from the box.

admirer	~~brother~~	day
deal (x2)	headed	money
shame	time	uncle	view

a I always used to argue with my
___big brother___ but now we
get on really well.

b Wow! What a _____
you've got from this balcony.

c Please don't worry about losing
that umbrella. It's no
_____ , really.

d Josh has been so _____
_____ since he came top of
the class in his exams.

e You've got a _____
tomorrow, so try and get to bed
early tonight.

f That's my _____ .
He's eighty-six years old, but
sometimes he acts like a
teenager!

g It's wonderful to meet you: I've
always been a _____
of your work.

h Thank you for showing me
round the city today. I had a
_____ .

i It's a _____ that
Virginia can't be with us today
to accept her award in person.

j My brother's working in the
City now, and making really
_____ .

k The department is under a
_____ of pressure to
finish this project by the end of
the month.

MODULE 9

Vocabulary
Strange events

1 a Read the following extracts from TV/radio programmes. Complete the gaps with words or phrases from page 96 of the Students' Book.

1 " On tonight's edition of 'Too w <u>e</u> i <u>r</u> <u>d</u> to be true?' we bring you the a _ _ z _ _ _ story of the woman whose p _ _ m _ _ _ _ _ _ _ of a bus crash saved the lives of fifty children, as well as reports of a m _ _ _ c _ _ in the Italian seaside village of Maiori, where the face of a saint appeared in the sand. "

2 " For those of you who like reading g _ _ s _ _ s t _ _ _ _ _ _ , this is a must. The book opens with a young woman discovering that a lady she sits next to on the bus knew her late mother. A series of further c _ _ _ c _ _ _ _ _ _ _ _ lead the heroine to a strange house in the country. The last few chapters are really s _ _ _ k _! "

3 " Six weeks after the m _ _ _ _ _ _ _ s d _ _ _ p _ _ _ _ _ _ _ _ of James Cogan from his home in Leeds, police are investigating links between this case and three u _ _ _ _ v _ _ m _ _ d _ _ _ in the north-west over the last five years. "

4 " Finally on the show tonight, an incredible story about a ten-year-old chess champion who uses t _ _ _ p _ _ _ _ to beat all his opponents. Young Damien Wilde claims to be able to see into other people's minds, and he'll be demonstrating his special powers on the programme tonight. "

5 " After the break we'll be discussing a rather d _ _ _ _ _ _ _ _ _ g c _ s _ o _ m _ _ _ _ k _ _ i _ _ _ _ _ _ y in California, where a young woman was held in police custody for over a week before being released. This is the second case of its kind in two months, and the public are demanding answers from the police. "

6 " The local council have dismissed as 'r _ _ _ c _ _ _ _ _' claims about crop circles appearing in the area, and say the episode was an elaborate h _ _ _ . "

7 " Although police were s _ _ _ _ _ _ _ _ _ about McKellen, and had noticed him acting strangely in the days following the murder, they didn't bring him in for questioning and by the time they acted he had already fled. 'It's d _ _ _ _ _ c _ _ _ _ ,' said local resident Betty White. 'How can you feel safe when you know the police have let a murderer escape?' "

b T9.1 Listen and check.

Modals and related verbs

2 Choose the correct alternative.

a If you like, I *can / may* make an appointment for you to see Dr Krall tomorrow.

b Passengers *mustn't / don't have to* smoke while on board the plane.

c Don't let Sylvie climb that tree. She *can / might* fall.

d You probably *shouldn't / mustn't* keep your passport in that pocket: it *should / could* easily be stolen.

e I'm afraid Karen *can't / couldn't* come to the party tomorrow because she's got flu.

f Oh no! It *mustn't / can't* be seven o'clock already! Jill and Graham will be here in fifteen minutes!

g I absolutely *ought to / have to* leave the house at six if I want to be at the station by six-thirty.

h Be careful, that pot's very heavy. You *have to / could* hurt your back.

3 a Replace the phrases in bold with a modal verb phrase. Sometimes there is more than one possible answer.

1 Is it true that cats **are able to** see in the dark?
_____can_____

2 **It's necessary for you to** wear sunscreen when you go to the beach. _____

3 **It's impossible for it to** be that expensive. **I'm sure there's** a mistake. _____

4 Do you think **it's the right thing for me to** buy Alex a birthday present? _____

5 The doctor said **I'm not allowed to** lift anything heavy. _____

6 **It's possible that we'll** be a bit late tonight.
_____

7 **It's not necessary for you to** join the team if you don't want to. _____

8 Frank's not in his office. I suppose **it's possible that he's** at lunch. _____

9 Come on, put those books away – **it's not a good idea for you to** be studying at this time of night.
_____

10 **Am I allowed to** have tomorrow off? **It's necessary for me to** go to the dentist.
_____

b Complete these sentences so that they are true for you.

1 I can _____ .
2 I can't _____ .
3 Tomorrow I may _____ .
4 This week I ought to _____ .
5 Tomorrow I have to _____ .
6 Tonight I might _____ .

4 Complete the conversations with an appropriate modal verb. Sometimes there is more than one possible answer.

a A: Is it possible to do colour copies on this printer?
 B: Well you _____can_____ , but it takes ages.

b A: Do you think it'll snow tonight?
 B: It _____ . It's suddenly got very cold.

c A: Don't you think you'd better see someone about your toothache?
 B: I know I _____ , but I hate going to the dentist.

d A: Isn't that your boyfriend over there with Susie?
 B: It _____ be! He's supposed to be in Paris on business!

e A: Do I really need to speak Spanish for the job?
 B: Well, you _____ , but it helps.

f A: Are the car keys in your jacket pocket?
 B: Well, they _____ be, unless someone's taken them.

g A: Come inside now – it's getting dark!
 B: Oh _____ we? We're in the middle of a game.

Wordspot
wrong

5 a Put the word *wrong* into these sentences, then match them with sentences a–i to make conversations.

1 `g` Oh, there's something *wrong* with it: it won't send text messages.
2 ☐ Let me have a look ... no, there's nothing with it, it just needs cleaning.
3 ☐ Oh sorry, I've got the number.
4 ☐ Well, it looks beautiful, but you're holding it the way up.
5 ☐ It's not like you to stay in on a Saturday night. What's?
6 ☐ No, you've got it on the way round.
7 ☐ Yes, I must admit I was about him.
8 ☐ At the mechanic's. The air conditioning system's gone again.
9 ☐ It's just that you always put everything in the place.

a Hello, 354667..., hello?
b Is this skirt supposed to have pockets at the front?
c Why don't you want me to help tidy up?
d I think I'll just stay in and watch TV.
e I don't think this mouse is working properly.
f Where's your car?
g Why aren't you using your new mobile phone?
h What do you think of this picture we bought at the exhibition?
i Gary's really quite interesting when you get to know him, isn't he?

b ⬛ T9.2 Listen and check.

65

Past modals

6 **a** Cross out the modals which do not fit in the sentences below. Sometimes you only need to cross out one.

1 Look, the river's frozen! It *must have been* / ~~*should have been*~~ / ~~*can't have been*~~ very cold during the night.

2 A: I think Greg's out. He didn't answer the phone.

B: But he *might not have heard* / *couldn't hear* / *may have heard* it – he sometimes plays his music very loud.

3 A: Here, I brought you some flowers.

B: Oh, you *shouldn't have done* / *didn't have to do* / *couldn't have done* that.

4 Sally! Look where you're going when you cross the road. You *must have been* / *could have been* / *might have been* hit by a car!

5 At school we *could learn* / *had to learn* / *managed to learn* two languages if we wanted to.

6 A: I'm very sorry I'm late, I got stuck in traffic.

B: Well you *could have called* / *must have called* / *should have called* to let us know. We've been waiting for half an hour.

A: I was going to phone, but I *couldn't find* / *can't have found* / *couldn't have found* the number.

b ◖T9.3◗ Listen and check. Then listen again and repeat, paying attention to the stressed words.

Past modals in everyday conversations

7 Use the prompts to write complete sentences.

A

PETE: Oh no! I / lose / my wallet.

Oh no! I've lost my wallet.

SUE: Where / last / have it?

PETE: I / not know. I / use / last night when I / buy / train ticket so I / must / have it then.

SUE: you / use it / since then?

PETE: No. I suppose / might / lose it on / train or / I might / leave it / home this morning.

SUE: Why / you / phone home / check?

B

STEVE: Where / you / be? / It / be / eleven o'clock!

ZENA: I / get / stuck / traffic.

STEVE: Well, you / should / phone!

ZENA: I / be / sorry, I / leave / mobile phone / home.

STEVE: But if I / know / you / be / late / I could / go / pub.

ZENA: I / be / really sorry.

8 Vanessa, Georgina, Mike and Gavin are students who share a student house. They often have arguments. Complete the gaps with the past form of one of the modal verbs *should*, *ought to*, *must*, *can't*, *might*, or *could* (positive or negative), and an appropriate verb.

VANESSA: Someone forgot to lock the front door last night.

MIKE: Well, it (a) ___can't have been___ me. I definitely remember locking it, so it (b) _____ someone who came home after me.

GEORGINA: You slept in the garden all night! Why didn't you wake us up?

GAVIN: Well, I rang the bell for ages, but no one answered. You (c) _____ to bed.

GEORGINA: Oh, you idiot. You (d) _____ a stone at the window.

GEORGINA: Vanessa and Gavin aren't speaking to each other this morning.

MIKE: They (e) _____ an argument. I remember hearing shouting last night.

VANESSA: Who's this?

MIKE: It's just my friend, Bill.

VANESSA: Well, you (f) _____ us that you were bringing someone home. I just sat on him!

GEORGINA: Oh no! Where have my chocolates gone? There are only two left!

VANESSA: Well, I think the cat (g) _____ them because I forgot to feed him, or it (h) _____ Gavin, because you know what he's like when he's hungry!

GAVIN: Look at this – and Georgina still hasn't done the washing-up!

MIKE: Well she (i) _____ the note.

MIKE: You look terrible.

GAVIN: Yes, I feel really sick.

MIKE: Well, you (j) _____ Georgina's chocolates. It's your own fault.

Listen and read
Coincidences

9 a **T9.4** Listen to and/or read these stories and match the pictures to the stories. There are two pictures you do not need.

A

I work in a market in London, just at the weekends – I've got a second-hand book stall, and one day I was getting my stall ready when a lady came up and started looking at the books. She started chatting and telling me how she used to live in that part of London and how much it had changed since she'd last been in the area. While we were talking, I put out a book and she picked it up. 'Oh, *Grimm's Fairy Tales*,' she said, 'I had a copy of this when I was a child. I used to read it again and again.' She began flicking through it and I carried on laying out the books, and when I looked up she was just standing there shaking, and she'd gone completely white. 'But ... but ... this is my actual book,' she gasped, 'Look, it's got my name, Joan, in it. How on earth did you get it?' Then she told me how there'd been a terrible fire while her family were away on holiday, and the house had been burnt to the ground. She thought all her belongings had been destroyed. She pulled out her purse to buy the book from me, but I stopped her. 'No, no ... please accept it as a gift – it's such a wonderful story.' 5
10
15

B

I was walking along the road in Windsor where I live, when I heard a phone ringing in a phone box, and something prompted me to go in and pick it up. There was a voice at the other end saying, in a very businesslike way, 'Sorry to bother you at home, Julian, but I can't find that file you were working on. Do you remember where you put it?' It was Jasmine, who I work with at my office in London. I stopped her before she could go on. 'Jasmine, I'm in a phone box – how did you know I was here?' And she just said, 'Stop messing around, I'm really busy and I need that file.' I kept trying to convince her about where I was, but she just wouldn't believe me. Anyway, I told her where the file was, and then suddenly she interrupted me: 'Julian! Hang on a minute, I didn't dial your home phone number! I dialled the Windsor code, but then I dialled your security card number, which is next to your name in the book at work.' So somehow my security card number just happened to be the same number as the phone box that I was walking past. 5
10

C

A couple of years ago, we moved to an old house in the country and the man who lived there before had died, and we had to clear up a lot of his belongings. So we built a big bonfire at the end of the garden and took all the rubbish down there to burn. I'd just put a box full of stuff onto the fire, and I was standing chatting, when there was a bang, and I felt something hit the side of my head. I took my earring off and there was a bullet stuck in it, which had been on the fire and exploded. If I hadn't had the earrings on, it would've gone straight into my neck. And the scary thing was, the bullet had the letter 'J' on it – and my name's Jane – so it was as if this bullet was intended for me. 5
10

b Listen and/or read again and match the sentences to the stories. There are four sentences for each story.

1 She must have felt astonished when she put the phone down. __B__
2 The previous owner must have had a gun in the house. _____
3 He could have walked on without stopping. _____
4 She could have missed him if she'd come on a Friday. _____
5 She can't have been standing very far away from the fire. _____
6 She can't be living in the area now. _____
7 She must have been delighted with what she found. _____
8 'J' might have been the initial of the manufacturer's name. _____
9 The fire can't have destroyed everything. _____
10 She could have been killed. _____
11 Somehow he must have known the call was for him. _____
12 She can't have been concentrating. _____

c Can you remember words from the texts to complete these sentences? Try doing them without looking and then check your answers.

1 The man was getting his stall ___ready___ when the old lady came up.
2 She started to flick _____ a book.
3 He looked up and saw that she had _____ completely white.
4 Jasmine thought Julian was messing _____ at first.
5 She thought she had _____ his home number.
6 The number _____ to be the same number as the phone box.
7 The woman was clearing _____ the dead man's belongings.
8 She put a box full of _____ onto the bonfire.
9 She found a bullet _____ in the earring.

Real life
Saying what's wrong with things

10 Use the clues to find words or phrases from page 104 of the Students' Book in the word square.

J	M	I	S	S	I	N	G	P	U	U	K
W	V	S	E	U	Z	B	Q	N	N	O	M
S	V	W	X	I	Q	C	Q	X	P	R	Y
S	C	R	A	T	C	H	E	D	O	D	O
H	O	R	V	Z	U	A	U	W	W	E	Z
R	D	E	U	H	P	R	Q	O	B	R	X
U	T	W	R	O	N	G	S	I	Z	E	O
N	T	O	D	L	D	I	D	B	V	D	B
K	O	R	E	E	V	N	Y	F	K	Z	U
K	W	K	X	Y	P	G	S	I	D	M	R
Q	Y	E	E	P	Q	P	S	T	A	I	N
C	H	I	P	P	E	D	T	R	K	X	T
I	W	R	O	N	G	C	O	L	O	U	R

a Do you have any more jackets in this colour? This one's got a button m_issing_____.
b I don't know what's wrong with this phone: it doesn't seem to be c_____ .
c Excuse me, could you bring me another cup, please? This one's c_____ .
d You can't wear that shirt to work – look, it's got a green s_____ on the front.
e Oh dear, these shorts are a bit tight – they must have s_____ in the wash.
f These sunglasses are so s_____ , I don't know how you can see anything through them!
g I like the style, but the colour doesn't s_____ me – have you got it in blue?
h I bought this sweater here yesterday, but when I got home I found it's got a big h_____ in it where the price tag was attached.
i I'm sure this isn't the sandwich I o_____: it's got mayonnaise in it.
j You'll have to turn the volume up on the television. The remote control doesn't w_____ any more.
k Have you got any more batteries, Dad? These ones are the w_____ s_____ for the radio.
l That shirt's the w_____ c_____ for you – green would look better.

Vocabulary booster
Describing things that are odd or unusual

11 a Put a word from the box under each picture.

broken down	melted	a hole	inside out	a crack
a mark	~~upside down~~	torn	got stuck	

1

upside down

2

3

4

5

6

7

8

9

b Complete the conversations with words and phrases from part a.

1   A: Why is Emily late?
    B: Her car has _broken down_. She's waiting for the mechanic.

2   A: Can I help you?
    B: Yes, I'd like to buy this blouse but it's got _____ on it. Have you got another one?

3   A: Waiter! Please can I have another glass? This one's got _____ in it.
    B: Of course. I'll throw the damaged one away.

4   A: Did you enjoy your skiing holiday?
    B: No, we didn't! The temperature went up and all the snow _____ .

5   A: The traffic's very slow this morning.
    B: Yes, there was a bad accident on the motorway. A car was _____ on its roof but luckily no one was hurt.

6   A: Dave was a mess this morning – did you see him?
    B: Yes, he was wearing different coloured socks and his sweater was _____! I could read the label and the washing instructions!

LOOK!

We often use *bad / badly* and *slight / slightly* to show how much something is damaged:

	adjectives
• *It's **slightly***	*torn*
badly	*cracked*
	chipped

Notice: with *broken* and *melted*, we use *completely* not *badly*:

• *It's **completely***	*broken*
	melted

	nouns
• *It's got a **slight***	*tear*
bad	*crack*
	stain
	mark

Pronunciation
Consonant clusters

> **LOOK!**
> When you find it difficult to pronounce two or more consonants together, try starting with the last one. Listen to this example or say it aloud.
> chipped   /t – pt – ɪpt – tʃɪpt/

12 **a** **T9.5** Listen to these words and say them aloud.

chipped	burnt	shrunk
/tʃɪpt/	/bɜːnt/	/ʃrʌŋk/

scratched	doesn't
/skrætʃt/	/dʌznt/

b **T9.6** Here are some common consonant clusters. Listen to these groups of words and repeat them.

/skr/	/spr/
scratch	spring
describe	expression
tapescript	aspirin
ice cream	sprained

/spl/	/str/
split	stress
explain	strong
explode	string
explore	extremely

c **T9.7** Listen and repeat the sentences.

1 Oh no! I've scratched my new glasses.
2 I learnt lots of useful expressions in class today.
3 I'd like to stay longer and explore the city.
4 The seam's split on this jacket – I'll have to take it back.
5 How did you sprain your ankle?
6 I think Rob's under a lot of stress at the moment.

Improve your writing
An e-mail about a problem

13 **a** Craig bought a second-hand mobile phone on eBay (a website on the Internet for buying and selling things), but there are some problems with it. He wrote an e-mail to the seller, but some of the words and phrases he has used are too formal. Replace them with a less formal word or phrase from the box.

Dear Techkid 100

I'm writing about the mobile phone which I ~~purchased~~ *bought* from you last week. I'm afraid there are a couple of problems that I need to ask you to resolve.

First of all, I think the car charger has a defect, because it doesn't charge the phone properly. I have tried it in a friend's car, but it continued to malfunction. I know you said you hadn't used the charger, so maybe you didn't know about this problem.

The other thing is the leather case – are you sure it's the one that accompanied the phone when you bought it, because it appears to be intended for a different model. The holes are incorrectly positioned, so when I put it on the phone, all the numbers are obscured.

Please respond to me about this at your earliest convenience,

Yours sincerely

Craig Lewis

---

came with   sort out   as soon as you can   still didn't work   ~~bought~~
looks as if it's for   has got something wrong with it   get back to me
covered up   Best regards   in the wrong place

b Imagine that you bought something (e.g. clothes, jewellery, an electrical item) on eBay, but there are some problems with it. Write an e-mail to the seller, explaining the problem and asking them to sort it out.

71

Vocabulary
Getting together

1 **a** Use the clues to complete the grid with words from page 106 of the Students' Book.

¹G	U	E	²S	T	S

1   Some of the ____ had come all the way from Hong Kong just for the wedding.
2   I went to a ____ last night, and it was great to see so many of my ex-classmates. (2 words)
3   I have an important business meeting with some ____ this afternoon.
4   In 2000, we had a big street party with all our ____ .
5   Could you make an ____ for me to see Mr Ikegame some time tomorrow?
6   I'm trying to organise a little ____ for a few friends at my place on Saturday – can you come? (2 words)
7   All our friends and ____ are going to be at the wedding.
8   When Kristin passed her exams, we went out for a ____ at her favourite restaurant. (2 words)
9   Each member of the United Nations may send five ____ to the General Assembly.
10 Aaron moved into his new apartment months ago and he still hasn't had a ____ party. (2 words)
11 Uma and Carl have arranged a ____ for me with a friend of theirs – I'm really nervous about going. (2 words)
12 There have been angry demonstrations outside the building where the two presidents are having their ____ meeting.
13 Representatives from over a hundred countries attended the International Peace ____ in Geneva.
14 We have an important meeting tomorrow morning, and I'd like all staff to ____ .

b **T10.1** Listen and check.

Will and *going to*

2 Complete the conversations with *'ll* or *going to* using the verbs in brackets.

a A: Can I speak to Miss Beatty in accounts?
    B: Yes, I _____*'ll put*_____ (put) you through.

b A: My calculator's not working and I need it for the exam.
    B: Don't panic, I _____ (lend) you mine.

c A: You look very tired – you need a break.
    B: Yes, I _____ (have) two days off next week. Mr Brumfit agreed to it.

d A: We've got a bit of a problem, there's a strong smell of gas in the house.
    B: Right, madam, I _____ (send) someone round immediately.

e A: So what's the kitchen like?
    B: It's nice and big but it's a bit dark, so we _____ (paint) it yellow.

f A: Your exam results weren't very good, were they?
    B: I know, but I've decided I _____ _____ (work) much harder next year.

g A: Do you want to have a party for your twenty-first birthday?
    B: Oh I don't know. I _____ (think) about it.

h A: Have you decided what to do about the house?
    B: Yes. We _____ (not sell) it after all.

i A: Did you get an e-mail from the accounts department this morning?
    B: I don't know, I _____ (check) my inbox.

j A: Are you and Jason friends again yet?
    B: No, I _____ (never speak) to him again!

Going to and Present continuous for intentions and arrangements

3 In many situations you can use either the Present continuous or *going to*. In the following sentences cross out the Present continuous where it is **not** possible, because it is not something we can arrange.

a Paula *is going to become / ~~is becoming~~* a specialist in heart surgery when she finishes her training.

b I'm *going to have / having* a party on Saturday. Would you like to come?

c I'm *really going to enjoy / really enjoying* the concert tomorrow night.

d My husband's *going to see / seeing* the doctor on Friday.

e What time is your sister's plane *going to leave / leaving*?

f Who are you *going to meet / meeting* for lunch today?

g One day I'm *going to meet / meeting* the girl of my dreams.

h Peter keeps telling us he's *going to make / making* a million pounds before he's forty.

i We're *going to spend / spending* the holidays with some friends from Canada.

j When are you *going to learn / learning* some table manners?

Present simple

4 In four of the sentences below, the Present simple is not used correctly to talk about the future. Find the mistakes and correct them.

a What time does your train get in? ✓

b Everything on the menu sounds delicious, but I have the chicken risotto.

c You break that window if you're not careful.

d What are you going to do when you retire?

e The delegates arrive at six o'clock and the conference begins at seven-thirty.

f Wait a minute – I help you with those bags.

g As soon as I get home, I promise I phone you.

h I'll get some more steaks in case Jan and Ian stay for dinner.

Predictions

5 a Sharon is worried about a barbecue she is organising, and her friend Rhona is reassuring her. Put *S* next to Sharon's comments and *R* next to Rhona's.

1 I don't know why I decided to have a barbecue this afternoon, I _____ *bet* _____ it'll rain. __*S*__

2 I'm never _____ get these salads ready in time. ____

3 Slow down a bit! You're _____ cut yourself with that knife if you're not careful. ____

4 Stop worrying about the food. _____ it'll all taste wonderful. ____

5 These steaks _____ take a while to cook – they're really thick. Are you going to put them on the barbecue first? ____

6 _____ that half the people I've invited won't come. ____

7 Well, at least fifteen people have told me they're coming. And _____ some of your neighbours will turn up, too. ____

8 Marc said he'd bring me some extra chairs but he'll _____ forget. ____

9 People _____ to want plenty of soft drinks. Shall I get some more juice from the shop? ____

10 There's just so much to do. I'm _____ forget something. ____

b **Complete the sentences in part a with a word or phrase from the box.**

almost certainly	are likely	~~bet~~	certain to
going to (x2)	I'm sure (x2)	may well	
there's a good chance that			

Listen and read
Are you sitting comfortably?

6 a ⬛ **T10.2** Listen to and/or read the text about feng shui. Which paragraph tells you …

1 the best position in the house for the kitchen? ___
2 what feng shui is? ___
3 what to do now? ___
4 where you should position the cooker? ___
5 what the article is about? ___
6 how to organise your dining room? ___

b **Listen and/or read again and answer the questions.**

1 What is 'qi'?

_____

2 What have to be balanced for a place to have good feng shui?

_____

3 Are bright or neutral colours better for your dining room and why?

_____

4 If you don't want your dinner guests to stay too long, where should you put the dining table?

_____

5 Describe two ways in which plants can be used in feng shui.

_____

6 If you have nine guests, how many chairs should there be at the dining table?

_____

7 What could put a dinner guest in a bad mood?

_____

8 Where should your kitchen be if you live in Australia?

_____

9 Why is it a good idea to have two doorways in a dining room, but a bad idea to have a window above a cooker?

_____

10 Where might it be necessary to put a mirror in the kitchen and why?

_____

Are you sitting comfortably?

A Do you want to be sure that your dinner party will be a success? Our expert tells you how applying feng shui in the kitchen and dining room can help.

B Feng shui is a way of creating harmony between humans and our environment to enhance our well-being. An ancient Chinese theory of design and placement, feng shui grew from observations that people are affected positively or negatively by their surroundings, with some places being noticeably luckier, happier, healthier or more peaceful than others. The Chinese believe that everything that exists has 'qi' (universal energy) and, in turn, everything that has 'qi' has 'yin' (passive, feminine) qualities and 'yang' (active, masculine) qualities. 'Yin' and 'yang' are opposites and complementary - one cannot exist without the other. When we feel good about a place the Chinese would say it has good feng shui because the 'yin' and 'yang' are balanced.

C So how does this affect your dinner party? Well, let's look at the dining room first. The Chinese believe you should not be distracted from the food or company during a meal because eating feeds both the body and spirit. So don't make your dining room décor too eye-catching. If the dining table is too near the front door it is said that people will be preoccupied with what is going on outside, and that guests will eat and run. If attached to the living room or kitchen, make your dining room a separate space by using plants or screens to block distractions. Two doorways will let 'qi' flow in and out, but if there's only one, allow enough space around it for easy access.

- Chairs should be comfortable so diners take their time to eat, digest well, and communicate with each other.
- Ideally, chairs should have good back rests and arms, and should be placed with their backs to the wall rather than to the windows and doors.
- Dining chairs should be even in number because even numbers represent luck

and single chairs loneliness. Add an extra chair if you have an uneven number.

- A round table is best. The next choice is octagonal, and if you have a square or rectangular table make sure no one gets a corner! The negative 'sha qi' could cause digestive problems or bad temper.

D Of course, it is also important to consider the place where the food is prepared. The kitchen is regarded as the source of general well-being by the Chinese because food represents wealth. If you prepare food in a kitchen with good feng shui, the people who eat it will carry the benefits throughout the day. Your kitchen is best placed to one side of your house - preferably on the south or southeastern side in the northern hemisphere and the north or northeastern side in the southern hemisphere - not in the centre, which is associated with the earth element. The balance of 'yin' and 'yang' is vital here, where the two major elements are water ('yin') and fire ('yang'). Your kitchen should be light and airy with little clutter. You will find that indoor plants, window boxes or small shrubs outside the window will help it stay cool.

E The area around the kitchen door or directly opposite it is known as the area of disturbed 'qi' and is not a good place to put the cooker. Rather, place it where there is assembled 'qi' - diagonally across from the door - but do not place it under a window or skylight, because the energy will quickly leave the house. You should also position it so that your back is not to the door while cooking, otherwise you may be surprised by someone coming up behind you and this could affect the food. If you can't see a door, install a mirror behind the cooker, to give you plenty of warning and to help the flow of 'qi'.

F So now it's time to start reorganising your home. Follow these simple guidelines, and you're sure to have successful dinner parties every time!

Vocabulary booster
Communicating

7 **a** Match the two halves of the phrases.

1	be deep in	a	someone
2	join a chat	b	chat with someone
3	have a	c	up with a friend
4	text	d	well with someone
5	improve your	e	an e-mail to someone
6	keep in	f	room
7	have a lot	g	touch with someone
8	catch	h	conversation with someone
9	get on	i	communication skills
10	forward	j	in common with someone

b Complete the sentences with a phrase from part a.

1 Do you still _keep in touch_ with people you used to know at school?

2 Our boss is sending us on a course to _____ our _____ .

3 It'll be good to _____ with Josh at dinner tomorrow: I haven't seen him for a while.

4 I like Tina as a person, but I don't think we have _____ in _____ .

5 Look at Craig and Megan: they've only just met and they're already _____ in _____ .

6 I'm just going to phone Sameeneh to _____ a _____ about the wedding preparations.

7 Could you please _____ this _____ to all the other people on the team?

8 I didn't like Darrell at first, but we _____ really _____ now.

9 It's a strange experience when you first _____ a _____ – like talking to lots of invisible people.

10 If you don't stop _____ your friends instead of doing your homework, I'm going to take that phone off you.

c **T10.3** Listen and check.

Future simple, perfect or continuous

8 **a** Circle the best verb form.

1 Do you think you *'ll still work /* (*'ll still be working*) */ 'll have worked* for Nabuko in five years' time?

2 Ten o'clock's fine: the meeting *will already start / will already be starting / will already have started*, but it doesn't matter if you come in late.

3 I'm afraid we can't use the school hall on Saturday afternoon. The decorators *won't finish / won't be finishing / won't have finished* by then.

4 Your uncle will be exhausted when he arrives because he *'ll drive / 'll be driving / 'll have driven* all the way from London.

5 Don't phone before two because we *'ll still have / 'll still be having / 'll still have had* lunch.

6 Don't worry, I'm sure Dr Jensen *will know / will be knowing / will have known* the answer.

7 I *'ll go / 'll be going / 'll have gone* past the supermarket on my way home from work anyway, so I can pick up some wine then.

b Correct the mistakes with future forms in these dialogues.

A (*2 mistakes*)

SECRETARY: When your plane gets in next Monday, a representative from our company, Mr Hashimoto, will be waiting for you.

MS JENKINS: How will I ~~be recognising~~ *recognise* him?

SECRETARY: He's quite tall and he'll have held a sign with your name on it. If you have any problems, just phone us immediately.

B (*1 mistake*)

MRS GUNNER: I'm almost sick with worry.

TANIA: What time's Henry's operation?

MRS GUNNER: At three o'clock this afternoon.

TANIA: I'll be thinking of you both then. I'm sure it'll have been okay.

MRS GUNNER: I hope so.

C (1 mistake)

ROB: I need to get this disk to Anne as soon as possible. Will you be seeing her today?

RIKKI: Yes, we've got a meeting with the sales department today at three-thirty. I'll be giving it to her then.

ROB: Thanks.

D (2 mistakes)

JACKIE: Will you be finishing your final exams by this time next week?

ELEANOR: Yes, by next Friday it'll all be over, thank goodness, and I'll have been my normal self again.

Pronunciation
Reading aloud: linking

> LOOK!
>
> When we speak, we link words in these ways:
>
> * *I put on the light.*
>   consonant → vowel
>   We pronounce **put on** as one word.
>
> * *He arrived last week.*
>   st → consonant
> * *He left the next day.*
>   xt → consonant
>   We don't pronounce the **t**.
>
> * *Richard had a good day.*
>   consonant → same consonant
>
> We don't make separate sounds, we hold the sound a little longer.

9 **a** **T10.4** Listen to the examples from the box and repeat them.

b Look at dialogues A and B in exercise 8b. Mark the links between the words and cross out any unnecessary *t* sounds.
e.g.
SECRETARY: When your plane gets in next Monday, a …

c **T10.5** Listen and repeat the dialogues, paying attention to the linking.

Future perfect or continuous

10 **a** Write complete sentences, using the Future continuous or perfect.

1 I / send nearly sixty e-mails by the end of today.
  I'll have sent nearly sixty e-mails by the end of today.

2 This time tomorrow, I / do my English homework and I / relax in front of the TV.
  _____
  _____

3 I / not / spend much time at home next weekend.
  _____

4 In two years' time I / lose some weight and I / give up smoking.
  _____
  _____

5 Six months from now I / live in a different country and I'll have a new job.
  _____
  _____

6 I / go out for a coffee with some friends later on today.
  _____
  _____

b Change the sentences so that they are true for you.

1 _____
  _____

2 _____
  _____

3 _____

4 _____
  _____

5 _____
  _____

6 _____
  _____

Improve your writing
Inviting a speaker

11 a You are organising your language school's Social Club and you are writing to invite the English manager of your local football team to speak one evening. Here are the notes you made before writing.

> *suggested dates: Wed 10th, 17th, 24th*
> *time: 7.30 p.m. (or later)*
> *speak for about an hour, incl time for questions*
> *fee?*
> *join us for dinner afterwards?*

You asked your teacher to look at the letter and she says there are fourteen grammatical mistakes in it! Find and correct the mistakes. The number of mistakes is given at the end of each line.

Dear Mr Gough

I'm writing

I ~~write~~ on behalf of my school club for ask if you would be able to come and give   2

us talk about your work with the team. Many of our member are keen fans and   2

would love hear about the training and opportunities for amateur footballers. We   1

have Social Club events all Wednesday evenings and we are looking for speakers   2

for 10th, 17th or 24th March.

If you are able to come, I suggest the talk to start at 7.30 (later if you wish, of   1

course) and lasts about an hour, including time for people ask questions. Also,   1

we are delighted if you would join us for dinner after.   2

Please let us to know which date would suit you, and what would be your fee.   2

I do hope you will be able to come. I look forward to hear from you.   1

Yours sincerely,

....

---

b Without looking back at the letter, decide if these words are spelt correctly. Write the correct spelling of any that are wrong on the line below.

1 behalf

_____

2 oppurtunities

_____

3 ameteur

_____

4 social

_____

5 event

_____

6 includeing

_____

7 delighted

_____

8 suit

_____

9 foward

_____

10 sincerly

_____

c Write a letter to invite a local English businessperson or celebrity to give a talk at your school. Start by writing notes, as in the example in part a.

_____

_____

_____

_____

_____

_____

_____

_____

_____

_____

_____

_____

_____

Real life
Dealing with problems on the telephone

12 **a** Rearrange the words to make responses, then write them under the sentences below to make conversations. The first word of each response is underlined.

1 message – earlier – my – Madrid – left – a – <u>I</u> – flight – about – to
2 good – <u>When</u> – to – a – ring – would – time – be – ?
3 up – <u>Sorry</u> – breaking – you're
4 <u>I'll</u> – through – her – put – to – you – just
5 time – ringing – <u>Sorry</u> – I – bad – am – a – at – ?
6 please – up – <u>Could</u> – bit – you – a – speak – ?
7 to – Jude – <u>thanks</u> – getting – me – for – back
8 with – bear – my – just – you'll – me – <u>If</u> – ask – I'll – boss
9 postcode – confirm – and – name – just – I – your – <u>Can</u> – ?
10 your – regarding – at – <u>it's</u> – son's – school – behaviour

a A: I'm sorry, Mr Grady is busy at the moment. Could you ring back a bit later on?

   B: *When would be a good time to ring?*

b A: Hello, Flight Centre, how can I help?

   B: Well, _____

c A: Patrick? It's Jude Cummins here – sorry it's a bit late.

   B: Oh, _____

d A: Could I speak to Jacqui Middleton, please?

   B: Yes, _____

e A: Hello, this is Mrs Howard, Dan's mother – you wanted to speak to me.

   B: Yes, _____

f A: The only tickets we have left are (*crackle*) at $15 for (*crackle*) …

   B: _____

g A: The wedding menu? Now where did I put it? Should be here somewhere …. oops, now I've dropped everything and ….

   B: _____

h A: Could you check and see when my order was actually sent out?

   B: _____

i A: This is Shoreton's wholesale foods. Do you want to order anything this week?

   B: I'm not sure. _____

j A: We should have somebody with you by three o'clock.

   B: _____

   A: I said, we should have somebody with you by three.

b **T10.6** Listen and check.

MODULE 11

Vocabulary
Modern medical science

1 **a** Answer the questions using a word or phrase from Reading and vocabulary on pages 116 and 117 of the Students' Book.

1 Which **V** protects you against diseases?
_____vaccination_____

2 Which **C** involves making an exact copy of a plant or animal? _____

3 Which **C S** can help you to change your appearance? _____

4 Which **E** happens when you get rid of something completely? _____

5 Which **I** means 'living forever'?
_____

6 Which **J** means 'a good reason for doing something'? _____

7 Which **L E** is usually higher for women than for men? _____

8 Which **P** means 'done for the first time'?
_____

9 Which **P** is the noun from 'poor'?
_____

10 Which **R** would most older people like to do to their bodies? _____

11 Which **R** is another word for 'looking like'?
_____

12 Which **W**s do most people want to hide, or try to get rid of? _____

b T11.1 Listen and check.

2 **a** Complete the chart with the noun forms.

verb	noun
develop	development
predict	
eliminate	
replace	
discover	
alter	
clone	
remove	

b T11.2 Listen to the noun forms and mark the stress.

c Complete the sentences with a verb or noun from the chart.

1 Liposuction involves the ___removal___ of unwanted fat from certain parts of the body.

2 A _____ is not always an exact copy of the original animal.

3 Although scientists _____ powerful new antibiotics every year, we still do not have a cure for many diseases.

4 Nowadays it is quite common to have an operation to _____ a knee or hip joint.

5 Many Hollywood stars say they would never make any _____s to their bodies.

6 The _____ of the human genome is a huge step forwards in the treatment of disease.

7 It is difficult to make accurate _____s about the future of the world's health.

8 So far it has not been possible to _____ the risks and side effects associated with cosmetic surgery.

80

Talking about hypothetical situations in the present

3 a Put the words in order to make questions.

Celebrity chef
Maggie Ellis answers
our questions.

1 if – months – work – What – you – take – could –
you – off – would – six – do – ?
*What would you do if you could take six
months off work?*

2 would – do – you – leader – What – a – you –
world – if – became – ?
_____

3 body – What – you – if – could – part – would –
your – change – you – of – ?
_____

4 desert – If – live – a – island, – you – with – take –
on – would – what – you – had – to – you – ?
_____

5 you – fire – from – home – on – if – What – was –
it – rescue – your – would – ?
_____

6 could – you – places – with – choose – who – If –
anyone, – you – change – would – ?
_____

7 What – school – study – you – back – if – went –
you – would – to – ?
_____

8 weeks – live – if – to – only – What – you – would –
had – you – four – do – ?
_____

b Complete the answers with the correct form of
the verbs in the box, then match them to the
questions in part a.

be (x2)	can (x2)	~~try~~	learn	want	love

a ☐ I _'d try_____ to make the gap between
rich and poor narrower.

b ☐ I'd save as many of my books as I
_____ .

c ☐ I'd eat and drink anything I _____ !

d ☐ If my children _____ a bit older, I'd
take them on a world tour.

e ☐ I think I'd take a camera, so I _____
record the experience.

f ☐ My hands – I _____ to have slim
elegant fingers.

g ☐ I _____ Italian, so I could read all
those wonderful old Italian recipe books.

h ☐ If it _____ just for a day, I'd choose
a supermodel!

c **T11.3** Listen and check.

d Write answers to the questions that are true for
you.

1 _____
_____

2 _____
_____

3 _____
_____

4 _____
_____

5 _____
_____

6 _____
_____

7 _____
_____

8 _____
_____

I wish and If only

4 Use the prompts to write complete sentences.

a I wish / I have / curly hair.
  I wish I had curly hair.

b If only I / can / drive.
  _____

c I wish Sally / speak up. I can hardly hear her.
  _____

d If only we / be / still on holiday.
  _____

e If only I / not get / so nervous before exams.
  _____

f I wish you / shut up / and / listen / to me.
  _____
  _____

It's time

5 Rewrite these sentences so that they have the same meaning, using *It's time*.

a Susan ought to get a job.
  It's time Susan got a job.

b We'd better go home now.
  _____

c The children should be in bed now.
  _____

d Jo should realise that money doesn't grow on trees.
  _____
  _____

e Why don't you learn to cook for yourself!
  _____

f I must buy myself a new watch.
  _____

g Why don't people do more to protect our environment?
  _____
  _____

h We should have more women in the government.
  _____
  _____

Pronunciation
/ə/

6 **a** Underline the vowels which are pronounced /ə/ in the words below. Sometimes there is more than one.

1 doctor
2 operation
3 medical
4 poisoning
5 discovery
6 swollen
7 alteration
8 poverty
9 temperature
10 removal
11 surgeon
12 development

b **T11.4** Listen and repeat the words, paying attention to the /ə/ sound.

Listen and read
Our health and wellbeing: facts or myths?

7 **a** **T11.5** Listen to and/or read the extracts about health and wellbeing. Are these statements true (T) or false (F)?

1 Coffee beans contain more caffeine than tea leaves.
  _____

2 Chocolate makes you live longer. _____
3 The best time to exercise is in the early evening.
  _____

4 You can get a cold from going out in the rain.
  _____

5 People who are allergic to pets are allergic to their fur. _____

b Listen and/or read again and answer the questions. What ...

1 should you eat three times a month?
  _____

2 is 'dander'? _____

3 might keep you awake at night? _____

4 makes about eighty cups of coffee?
  _____

5 cause colds and flu? _____

Researchers at Harvard University, in the US, studied 8,000 men for 65 years and found those who ate modest amounts of chocolate up to three times a month lived almost a year longer than those who didn't eat any. They concluded that this was likely to be because cocoa contains antioxidants called polyphenols, also found in red wine, which prevent the oxidation of harmful cholesterol. Antioxidants are also known to protect against cancer.

Although getting caught in the rain may make you feel cold and uncomfortable, this unpleasant experience will not in itself cause you to catch a virus. As the viruses that cause colds and flu are spread by tiny moisture droplets, you can only catch a cold or flu by:

- breathing in moisture droplets carrying the viruses (often as a result of an infected person coughing or sneezing near you) or;

- shaking hands with or touching an infected person.

More people seem to catch colds and flu in cold weather because they spend a lot of time indoors together and are therefore more likely to come into contact with viruses. Make sure you wash your hands frequently and stand back from people with coughs and sneezes.

There are all kinds of popular theories: that first thing in the morning is best because you will speed up your metabolism and burn more calories all day; that exercising before dinner will reduce your appetite; that exercise in the evening won't work because it will rev you up and keep you from getting a good night's sleep. However, many experts agree that our body temperature plays an enormous part in exercise and fitness performance, and that the body performs best when its temperature is naturally higher, which is at around six p.m. Muscular temperature also affects our flexibility and strength, so we are less likely to injure ourselves at that time of day, and more likely to be able to develop a muscular physique.

It depends on whether you are referring to the loose product or the brewed cup. Tea leaves have more caffeine than coffee beans before they are brewed. Prepared, however, tea is diluted quite a bit more than most coffees: a pound of tea yields 200 – 250 cups of tea while a pound of coffee makes approximately eighty cups. This will of course vary depending on how strong you like your tea or coffee. It has also been found that about eighty percent of the caffeine content in tea is extracted during the first minute of brewing. So if you want to reduce your caffeine intake, one suggestion is to discard the first brew and then make another cup using the same teabag or tea leaves.

A dog may be a man's best friend, but not if the man is among the estimated ten to fifteen percent of the population that suffers from pet allergies. The allergen is a specific protein produced not in the animal's fur, but primarily in its skin and – to a lesser extent – its saliva. As the animal is stroked or brushed, or as it rubs up against furniture or people, microscopic flakes of skin (called dander) become airborne. Since all cats and dogs have skin, there are no non-allergenic breeds.
However, since short-haired pets have less hair to shed, they send less dander into the air, so are preferable for those with pet allergies. Dogs are half as likely to cause allergic reactions as cats, but if you're allergic to furry animals, the only no-risk pets are fish and reptiles.

c **Answer the questions.**

1 Why are we less likely to injure ourselves if we exercise at around six p.m.?

_____

_____

2 If you are allergic to animals, is it best to have a dog or a cat as a pet?

_____

3 Can you catch a cold by shaking hands with someone?

_____

4 How are chocolate and red wine similar?

_____

_____

5 If you want less caffeine from your tea, should you drink it immediately or make a second brew?

_____

Vocabulary booster
Illness and injury

8 a Answer the questions. Use a dictionary if necessary.

1 **antibiotics, painkillers**
Which cures infections?
_____antibiotics_____

2 **a rash, a blister**
Which can you get if your shoes are too tight? _____

3 **take your temperature, take your pulse**
The doctor might hold your wrist to do this: _____

4 **dizzy, faint**
How do you feel if you have difficulty balancing? _____

5 **have an injection, have an operation**
Which do you usually have an anaesthetic for?
_____

6 **indigestion, food poisoning**
Which is often caused by eating too fast?
_____

7 **a blood test, a blood transfusion**
Which do you have to find out what is wrong with you?
_____

8 **itchy, swollen**
Which describes the way your skin feels when you want to scratch it?
_____

9 **sneeze, choke**
Which do you do when your throat is blocked? _____

10 **a bandage, a plaster cast**
Which one can people write messages on? _____

b **T11.6** Listen and check.

Talking about hypothetical situations in the past

9 Complete the sentences with the correct form of one of the verbs in the box (negative or positive).

| ask | be | ~~call~~ | get | go | know | listen | look |
| mention | miss | notice | offer | tell (x2) | wake | | |

a Thank you for your help last night: if you
_____hadn't called_____ the police so quickly, there might _____ a fight.

b I wish you _____ me about the surprise party for Marta – I'm no good at keeping secrets!

c A: Please don't wake me up too early tomorrow, Mum.
B: Look, if I _____ you at six this morning, you would _____ the train!

d Why did you tell Josef about the scratch on the car? If you _____ it, he _____ anything!

e A: I wish I _____ my boss that I can speak Korean.
B: Why not?
A: Well, then he wouldn't _____ me to translate all these boring documents.
B: But he wouldn't _____ to send you on a marketing trip to Seoul, either!

f A: If you _____ about the storm, _____ you _____ sailing?
B: No! I wish I _____ at the weather forecast.

g If only Nathan _____ to my advice – I'm sure he would _____ the job.

10 In these hypothetical situations, complete the two possible endings (one about the present and one about the past) with the correct form of the verbs in brackets.

a If Julie and Sam hadn't had that terrible row,

1 they _wouldn't have split up_ .

2 they _____ together now.

(not split up / still be)

b If the banks had been more honest,

1 we _____ in such a mess.

2 the stock market _____ .

(not be / not collapse)

c If Ed had given up smoking ten years ago,

1 he _____ such bad asthma now.

2 he _____ hundreds of pounds.

(not have / save)

d If I'd worked harder at school,

1 I _____ my exams.

2 I _____ a better job.

(pass / have)

e If Tammi had made a back-up copy of her files,

1 she _____ them all.

2 she _____ them now.

(not lose / not retype)

Using auxiliaries with *I wish* and *If only*

LOOK!

> In conversation we often just use an auxiliary instead of repeating the verb:
>
> • *Can you play the piano?*
>   *No, but I wish I could play the piano.*
>
> • *Did you watch* First Sight *on television last night?*
>   *No, but I wish I had watched it. Everybody said it was great.*

11 Complete the gaps with the correct auxiliary verb (e.g. *did, didn't, would, wouldn't, had, hadn't, could, couldn't*).

a A: Has Jim applied for the director's job?

B: Yes, but now he wishes he _hadn't_ . He doesn't really want all that extra responsibility.

b It's a pity you didn't come to the party.

Yes I wish I _____ . I didn't get anything done at home.

c A: I'm thinking of doing a computer course.

B: I wish you _____ . It might mean you could leave that awful job of yours.

d A: Did you bring any water?

B: No, I wish I _____ . I didn't realise it would be so hot.

e A: Will Sally be able to come to dinner?

B: No, she wishes she _____ but she's got to revise for her exams.

f A: You're under thirty, aren't you?

B: I wish I _____ ! No, I'm thirty-five.

g A: Are you going to the school play tonight?

B: Yes, but I wish I _____ . I'm absolutely exhausted and I just want to collapse in front of the TV.

Real life
Giving and reporting opinions

12 Insert a missing word from the phrases on page 121 of the Students' Book into each sentence below.

a Many people would *say* that the government should cut taxes.

b I haven't really ___ about it, but I suppose I'd vote for the Green party.

c I ___ absolutely convinced that the government will win the next election.

d All politicians are dishonest, ___ you ask me.

e As far ___ I'm concerned, this government is doing a good job.

f I've ___ doubt that some people are corrupted by power and status.

g I think politics is boring, ___ be honest.

h Although it's said that the government is out of touch, I don't agree.

Improve your writing
Reporting opinions

13 **a** The report below was written by a student who collected opinions about one of the questions on page 124 of the Students' Book. What is the purpose of each paragraph in the report?

A _____

B _____

C _____

D _____

b How many arguments were given in favour of the statement, and how many were given against it?

In favour: _____

Against: _____

c Complete the gaps in the report with a word from the box.

> argued   argument   gave
> opposed   point   strongly
> suggested   ~~summarise~~

d Collect other students' opinions on another question from page 124 of the Students' Book. Write a report on your findings, like the one in part a.

Too young to change?

A   The purpose of this report is to (1) ____summarise____ students' opinions about the following statement: people should be allowed to have cosmetic surgery before the age of eighteen. Information was collected via a survey of fifty students from different classes in the school.

B   About twenty percent of those interviewed for this survey (2) _____ arguments in favour of the statement. Some people felt that if a child was disfigured in some way, and was being bullied at school, then cosmetic surgery would be justified. Another (3) _____ was that surgery may sometimes be necessary for medical reasons, for example if a person cannot breathe because of the shape of their nose. A few people also made the (4) _____ that if someone is old enough to drive or get married at sixteen, then they should be able to decide for themselves about cosmetic surgery.

C   However, many people (5) _____ against the statement, the most common reason being that an impressionable teenager may make a decision because of peer pressure, then regret it later in life. Some people (6) _____ that young people would not be able to cope with the risks and possible side effects connected with cosmetic surgery. Most of those interviewed felt (7) _____ that society should not encourage young people to see appearance as more important than anything else.

D   In conclusion, it appears that the vast majority of students are (8) _____ to the idea of cosmetic surgery under the age of eighteen.

Vocabulary
TV programmes

1 **a** Read these comments from a survey, which asked, 'Do you think the quality of TV programming has got worse in recent years?' Complete the gaps with a word or phrase from pages 126–127 of the Students' Book.

1
> I don't think so: I saw a really i n f o r m a t i v e d _ _ _ _ _ _ _ _ _ about dolphins the other week, and there's an excellent c _ _ _ s _ _ _ on Sunday evenings at the moment, which has some really interesting guests on it.

2
> *Definitely. The only thing that's w _ _ _ _ _ watching nowadays is the n _ _ _ , and even that's often just too depressing!*

3
> Yes, I do. What I hate most these days are all the c _ _ _ _ s _ _ _ _ _ they put on – you know, murder mysteries, police thrillers, that sort of thing. They're full of v _ _ _ _ _ _ _ and bad language.

4
> Well, my husband hates all those American s _ _ _ _ _ _ , but I think he just doesn't understand the jokes! I mean, they're just h _ _ _ _ _ _ s fun, really, aren't they?

5
> *No. I watch a lot of football and I think that l _ _ _ s _ _ _ _ _ c _ _ _ _ _ _ _ is much better than it used to be: you don't miss any of the action. The only thing is that there are far too many t _ _ _ _ _ _ _ _ _ c _ _ _ _ _ _ _ _ _ _ these days. Sometimes they seem to come on every ten minutes or so.*

6
> No not at all! I'm a big fan of afternoon s _ _ _ _ . I get really involved in the lives of the characters, and I find them completely a d _ _ _ _ _ _ _ : I can't bear to miss an episode.

7
> I don't know if it's got worse, but there should be more c _ _ _ _ _ _ _ like *The Simpsons* and other programmes a _ _ _ d a _ young people.

8
> *It depends on the channel. There's a very good c _ _ _ _ _ _ _ _ a f _ _ _ _ _ _ programme called 60 minutes on ABC during the week: the producers aren't afraid to deal with quite c _ _ _ _ _ _ _ _ _ _ _ _ topics, and the reporting is a lot less b _ _ _ s _ _ than on some other news programmes.*

b **T12.1** Listen and check.

Vocabulary booster
The media

2 **a** Circle the word which does not belong in each category.

1 People who work for TV:
presenter, news reader, sports commentator, game show host, viewer

2 Adjectives to describe magazines:
glossy, quarterly, special interest, daily, teen

3 Sections of a newspaper:
domestic news, editorial, listings, headlines, obituaries

4 Things you can do with a radio:
tune in to a station, adjust the brightness, listen to live music, turn up the volume, listen to a phone-in

5 People who work for a newspaper:
editor, reporter, make-up artist, cartoonist, reviewer

6 Types of book:
a novel, a biography, a manual, a feature, a travel guide

7 Adjectives for criticising the media:
biased, offensive, thoughtful, intrusive, inaccurate

b Complete the sentences with a word from part a.

1 Look in the _____listings_____ at the back of the paper to see where the film is on.

2 Thousands of people _____ to Radio 4 to listen to JK Rowling reading extracts from *Harry Potter*.

3 I've got to have a meeting with the _____ in a minute to discuss the feature I'm writing about Tasmania.

4 I've lost the instruction _____ for my phone: do you know how to send picture messages?

5 Did you watch the music awards last night? The _____ was terrible – he kept forgetting people's names!

6 Have you read this article about experiments on animals? It's incredibly _____ – it doesn't give the other side of the argument at all.

7 *Cycling Weekly*? It's over there on the middle shelf, with all the _____ magazines.

c T12.2 Listen and check.

Reporting people's exact words

3 **a** Tick the comments below that are compliments.

1 Michael told me that I've got beautiful eyes. ✔
   You've got beautiful eyes.

2 Julie said that she admired my honesty.

3 Maddy said that I had cheated in the exam.

4 Carrie said that she wants to get her hair cut like mine.

5 Marcia and Paul said they wouldn't be late.

6 Tom said I looked as if I'd lost weight.

7 My boss told me that he was going to reduce my salary.

8 Tina said it was a long time since she'd eaten such delicious food.

b Write the people's exact words.

4 Complete the dialogues, using information from the speech bubbles.

I've been to New Orleans.

The room will cost £40.

It's going to rain.

The food at the Pizza Parlour is terrible.

I don't want an ice cream, thank you.

I've posted the letter to Sachs & Co.

Mr Cooper will be free at three o'clock.

You've got plenty of time to get to the airport.

a A: Why are you wearing a raincoat?
   B: They said on the radio that *it was going to rain* .

b A: I'd love to visit New Orleans.
   B: I thought you said _____ _____ .

c A: Oh, didn't you get me an ice cream?
   B: But you said _____ _____ .

d A: That's £50 for the room, including breakfast.
   B: But I was told _____ _____ .

e A: I'm afraid Mr Cooper's in a meeting.
   B: But when I spoke to you earlier, you said _____ _____ .

f A: I can't find the letter to Sachs & Co. anywhere.
   B: But you told me just now that _____ _____ .

g A: Let's go to the Pizza Parlour for lunch.
   B: But I thought you said _____ _____ .

h A: Come on – you'd better get a taxi or you'll miss your flight.
   B: But they told me at reception _____ _____ .

Wordspot
speak and *talk*

5 Put a word from the box into the correct place in each sentence to make phrases with *speak* or *talk* from page 131 of the Students' book.

about	actions	mind	~~peace~~	point	radio
shop	show	small	terms	to	up	well

a After six hours, there has been very little progress in
   peace
   the/talks between the two sides.

b Is that Frank? You're on *Eastern Suburbs Talk* – what's your question for the team?

c I've never met Stephanie, but Robert's always spoken very of her.

d What's worrying you, Todd? Come on, you're not usually afraid to speak your.

e Are you and Paula on speaking again yet?

f Do we have to go to the party? You know I hate making talk with Annie and Jeff's friends.

g Jon certainly knows what he's talking when it comes to choosing wine.

h You'll have to speak when you're giving your presentation – it's a very big room.

i I'm sorry to talk at the weekend, but I need to ask you about the Freeman report.

j At 9.30 we're showing ITC's new talk, hosted by comedian Dean Skinner.

k I wasn't talking myself, I was using the earpiece on my mobile phone – look!

l The national lottery scandal is a real talking all over the country at the moment.

m I bought her some flowers as a way of saying sorry. After all, 'speak louder than words,' as they say.

Pronunciation
Verbs that summarise what people say

6 a Mark the stress on the verbs below and circle the odd one out in each group (the verb which has a different stress pattern from the others).

   ● ● ●

1 admitted   (threatened)   insisted   suggested

2 warned   blamed   agreed   said

3 accused   refused   denied   apologised

4 suspected   reminded   explained   invited

5 offered   persuaded   promised   ordered

b **T12.3** Listen and check. Repeat the verbs.

Jazz chant

7 a Read the jazz chant and complete the gaps with the correct form of the verbs in brackets: infinitive, gerund or preposition + gerund.

Tom persuaded his mother (1) _to lend_ (lend) him
   her car
And promised (2) _____ (get) back by eight
His mother agreed (3) _____ (give) him the keys
And trusted him not to be late.
When the police brought him home at a quarter to two
She ran down the stairs from her bed
'We suspect this young man (4) _____ (tell) us lies'
She refused (5) _____ (believe) what they said.
She insisted (6) _____ (hear) his side of the tale
He admitted (7) _____ (drive) too fast
But strongly denied (8) _____ (have) too much
   to drink
'My first glass of beer was my last.'
The officers threatened (9) _____ (take) him away
His mum wouldn't let them and she
Suggested (10) _____ (discuss) the case the
   next day
They did, and they let him go free.

b **T12.4** Listen to the jazz chant and say it aloud.

Verbs that summarise what people say

8 **a** Six of the sentences below are wrong. Correct the mistakes, using verbs from the box.

threaten	agree	deny	refuse	blame	warn
complain	persuade	~~promise~~	assure	decide	

 promised
1 Simon ~~threatened~~ to bring Josie some expensive perfume from Paris.

2 The President refused having an affair with his secretary.

3 We're trying to persuade our boss to give us an extra day's holiday in the summer.

4 Tony accused the late nights at his office for the breakup of his marriage.

5 Paula wanted to drive home from the party, but we decided her to take a taxi.

6 Sonia suggested booking a table in case the restaurant got very busy.

7 The car dealer urged me that his prices were the lowest in town.

8 I'm sure we'd all like to congratulate André on winning the championship.

9 The company offered to double Jeremy's salary if he would stay on.

10 At the end of the evening, we concluded to meet the next day.

b Rewrite the sentences using a summarising verb from part a, so that they have the same meaning.

1 Let's hire a van and travel round Europe.

   He _suggested hiring a van and travelling around Europe_ .

2 No, I'm not going to pay.

   She _____ .

3 I didn't break the photocopier, honestly.

   She _____ .

4 This food is undercooked.

   She _____ .

5 Be careful Pat, the roads are very slippery.

   She _____ .

6 If you don't turn that noise down, I'm going to call the police.

   She _____ .

7 Would you like me to have a look at your TV?

   He _____ .

8 The misunderstanding was your fault, Geoff.

   She _____ .

Improve your writing
A letter of complaint

9 **a** Cecilia went on a day trip to Bath and Stonehenge in England. Look at the notes she made on the advertisement, then complete her letter to the company with a word or phrase from the box.

DAY TRIP TO
Bath and Stonehenge

arrived 40 minutes late

Sunday August 16th

only tours booked in advance — we hadn't booked!

10.00 We arrive in the historic city of Bath and tour the Roman Baths

11.30 Free time: taste the water from the underground springs and stroll through the old streets full of souvenir shops

too crowded, many shops closed

or

visit the Museum of Costume — *closed!* and admire the architecture of the Circus and Crescents *— not enough time to do this*

1.00 We go on to Stonehenge

touch the old stones – site of Druid sacrifices

can't touch the stones — all behind big wire fences

relax in the peace and quiet of the English countryside

5.00 We return to London

BARGAIN TOURS LTD, UK.

Dear Sir

I am writing (1) ___with regard to___ the day trip to Bath on Sunday August 16th, organised by your company. My friends and I were disappointed with the trip for several reasons.

(2) _____ , we arrived in Bath forty minutes late and (3) _____ had less time there than we had been told.

(4) _____ , the advert promised that we would tour the Roman Baths, but we found that a tour had not been booked for us.

(5) _____ , several places were closed, including some shops and the Museum of Costume.

(6) _____ , the advert suggested visiting the Circus and the Crescents, but we didn't have enough time.

(7) _____ the visit to Stonehenge, this was a further disappointment. Your advert claimed that we could touch the stones, (8) _____ they are actually behind big wire fences.

(9) _____ , we feel that the trip was not worth the £30 that we each paid, and we would appreciate some form of compensation for our disappointment.

I look forward to hearing from you,

Yours faithfully,

Cecilia Johnson

| therefore | all in all | ~~with regard to~~ | to begin with |
| secondly | in addition | whereas | as for |
| on top of all this |

b Imagine that you took some English visitors on a sightseeing trip to a place of interest in your country, but were disappointed. Write a letter to the UK tour organisers pointing out how the trip was different from their advertisement.

Think about these questions before you write:
- Were the times the same as in the advertisement?
- Were all the places open?
- Did you have to pay any extra money?
- Did you have enough time to see places?
- Were the descriptions of the places accurate?

Listen and read
So you want to write a best-seller?

10 a T12.5 Listen to and/or read the article. Put the tips about writing a best-seller in the correct places 1–9 in the text.

- Make your first page special.
- Expect rejection.
- Try to write something every day.
- Write a plan for your book.
- If you really want to do it, just start writing.
- Really target your agent.
- Don't be too possessive about your work.
- Research your market.
- Don't underestimate the power of the title.

b Listen and/or read again. Are these statements true (T) or false (F), according to the article?

1 Claudia Pattison thinks that anyone can write a book. _____

2 She used to be involved in celebrity journalism. _____

3 She earned at least £1,000,000 in advance for her first two books. _____

4 You need to know how the story is going to end before you start writing. _____

5 Stephen King never writes a plan for his books. _____

6 It's best not to waste time thinking about the title until after you've written the book. _____

7 Bloomsbury was the third publisher that JK Rowling sent her *Harry Potter* book to. _____

8 Agents and editors are useful because they have access to information that the writer doesn't have. _____

SO YOU WANT TO WRITE A BEST-SELLER?

They say everyone has at least one book inside them. But is it true? Could we all turn our hands to writing blockbusters for a living? Debut novelist Claudia Pattison shares her secrets for literary success.

Claudia Pattison, author of *Wow!* and *Fame Game*, believes we all have potential. And she should know. Claudia wrote *Wow!* – a satire on the world of celebrity journalism – in eight months, and was taken on by the second agent she met. Her very first book sparked a manic bidding war between rival publishers, and it's a sign of her potential that the winners, Pan Macmillan, offered a six-figure sum for a two-book deal – the average a debut author can usually expect is between £5,000 and £10,000.

'I really believe that everybody has a book in them,' says Claudia, who describes her genre as 'chick lit' – stories aimed at young women. 'I think the hardest thing is starting. You don't have to have a mad life or incredible experiences. You just need to be able to make different scenarios interesting.'

Claudia's tips on how to write a novel and get it published:

1 _____

_____

Claudia says: 'I knew chick lit was a growing arena and there was room in the market for more of the same, so I devoured every bit of it I could get my hands on. I also knew, however, that I couldn't just jump on the bandwagon; I needed to have a new spin. The obvious thing for me, with my background, was to write about celebrity journalism. If it all sounds very calculated, that's because it was. I thought about what would sell, and what would stand out in a crowd.'

2 _____

_____

Even if you're not sure what the plot is going to be or what comes next, just get something written down. Claudia says: 'What put me off originally was the idea that I had to have a clever plot. If you can just do good scenarios and interesting relationships, you're well on your way.'

3 _____

_____

If people aren't grabbed by the first page, they won't go any further.

4 _____

_____

Claudia says: 'Some people don't

phen King for one), but I think I
ld have found the whole task too
nting without one. I would've
cked.'

n if it's just three lines, it helps you
b in touch with the characters and
plot.

to think of something original and
k hard about it. Don't do it as an
rthought.

dia says: 'Look in the *Writers'*
Artists' Yearbook for brief
anations of specialities. Also, try
nd a book that you like or feel is
lar to yours. Many writers thank
r agents so you can find relevant
nts that way.' There's no point in
eting your crime book at an agent
specialises in romantic fiction.

Jewell, author of *Ralph's Party*,
t through nine agents before the
h saw her potential. *Harry Potter*
er JK Rowling was turned down
wo publishers before Bloomsbury
ped her up. Says Claudia, 'If you
ect it, you won't be disappointed.
t keep trying. Obviously, though, if
get twenty rejections all telling
there's no market for your book,
do have to take note.'

bu do get to the stage where you
e an agent or an editor, listen to
r advice. They have a wider
rview of the market and the
der gossip on what people are
ing for. They are the experts in
r field. 'I followed every bit of
ice,' says Claudia. 'I think the book
e million times better as a result.'

Improve your writing
Describing a book you have enjoyed

11 **a** The three circles below contain useful vocabulary for writing about a book. Match each title to a circle.

- *types of book*
- *adjectives to describe the writer*
- *adjectives to describe the story/book*

1 _____ 2 _____ 3 _____

Circle 1	Circle 2	Circle 3
fascinating	a detective story	great
moving	a romantic novel	skilled
brilliant	an adventure story	observant
hilarious	a science fiction novel	gifted
gripping	a historical novel	perceptive
well-written	a humorous story	entertaining
	a thriller	

b Complete the sentences below about a book you have read recently. Notice that there are three paragraphs: the introduction, the story, and your opinion, and that you need to use the Present simple for telling the story.

One of the best books I have read recently was
.... by ....
It is a .... (**type of book**) and I read it
because ....

It is set in .... (**place**), in
.... (**time**) and it is about ....
.... (**general topic**).

The story follows the relationship between ... **or** the events that
take place ... **or** the adventures of ....
....
At the beginning of the book, ...
....
then, ...
....
and at the end, ...
....

I found the book .... and I think
.... (**name of author**) is a really
.... writer. I'd certainly recommend it
to anyone who likes ....
....

Pronunciation table

Consonants		Vowels	
Symbol	**Key Word**	**Symbol**	**Key Word**
p	**p**an	iː	b**ea**t
b	**b**an	ɪ	b**i**t
t	**t**ip	e	b**e**t
d	**d**ip	æ	b**a**t
k	**c**ap	ɑː	b**ar**
g	**g**ap	ɒ	bl**ock**
tʃ	**ch**ur**ch**	ɔː	b**ough**t
dʒ	**ju**dge	ʊ	b**oo**k
f	**f**ew	uː	b**oo**t
v	**v**iew	ʌ	b**u**t
θ	**th**row	ɜː	b**ur**n
ð	**th**ough	ə	br**o**ther
s	**s**ip	eɪ	b**ay**
z	**z**ero	əʊ	b**o**ne
ʃ	fre**sh**	aɪ	b**y**
ʒ	mea**s**ure	aʊ	b**ou**nd
h	**h**ot	ɔɪ	b**oy**
m	su**m**	ɪə	b**eer**
n	su**n**	eə	b**are**
ŋ	su**ng**	ʊə	p**oor**
l	**l**ot	eɪə	pl**ayer**
r	**r**ot	əʊə	l**ower**
j	**y**et	aɪə	t**ire**
w	**w**et	aʊə	fl**ower**
		ɔɪə	empl**oyer**
		i	happ**y**
		u	ann**u**al

Special signs

/ˈ/ shows main stress

/ˌ/ shows secondary stress

/ə/ means that /ə/ may or may not be used

Pearson Education Limited
Edinburgh Gate
Harlow
Essex CM20 2JE
England
and Associated Companies throughout the world.

www.longman.com

First published 2005
Second impression 2006

ISBN-10: 0-582-82527-X
ISBN-13: 978-0-582-82527-7

Set in 9pt Stone Informal

Printed by Mateu Cromo, S.A. Pinto, Spain

Designed by Jennifer Coles

Project Managed by Lindsay White

Author Acknowledgements

The publishers and authors are very grateful to the following
people for reporting on the manuscript: Leslie Hendra,
International House, London; Sally Parry, United Int College,
London.

The publishers and authors would like to thank the following
people for their help and contribution:

Sarah Cunningham and Peter Moor for their ongoing
encouragement and advice; Jonathan Tennant and all at
International House Sydney for their encouragement and
support; Bill Eales and our colleagues at International House
London for their support; Jonathan Barnard, Rachel Bladon,
Jenny Coles, Jenny Colley, Sally Cooke, Yolanda Durham, Tina
Gulyas, Liz Moore, Sarah Munday, Ann Oakley, Alma Gray,
Shona Rodger, Lindsay White.

We are grateful to the following for permission to reproduce
copyright material:

Premier Holidays Ltd for an extract from a *Premier Holidays
Short Break* brochure; The Telegraph Group Limited for an
extract from the article 'Some handy tips about tipping' by
Rebecca Barrow published in *The Saturday Telegraph* 20th June
1998 © The Telegraph Group Ltd (1998); and Lansdowne
Publishing Pty Ltd for an extract from *Feng Shui: How to Create
Harmony and Balance in Your Living and Working Environment* by
Belinda Horwood © Lansdowne Publishing, Sydney.

In some instances we have been unable to trace the owners of
copyright material and we would appreciate any information
that would enable us to do so.

Photo Acknowledgements

We are grateful to the following for permission to reproduce
copyright photographs:

Every effort has been made to trace the copyright holders and
we apologize in advance for any unintentional omissions. We
would be pleased to insert the appropriate acknowledgement in
any subsequent edition of this publication.

Camera Press: page 63 top; Corbis: page 83 (Royalty Free);
Famous: page 8; Getty Images: page 7 (Image Bank), page 11
top and bottom, page 13, page 24 top and bottom, page 45
(Image Bank), page 61, page 63 bottom, page 85 top, page 91
bottom; Pictor: page 91 bottom; Rex Features: page 26 (Leon
Schadeberg), page 36 (Matt Baron/BEI), page 60 (Julian
Makey), page 62 (AXV); The Kobal Collection: page 18 top
(Amblin/Universal) left (Lucasfilm Ltd/Paramount) right
(Universal), page 39 (Warner Bros/DC Comics); Page 92 –
courtesy of Macmillan Publishers Limited

Illustrated by Colin Brown, Nicky Dupays, Conny Jude,
Tim Kahane, Sam Thompson (Eikon) and Theresa Tibberts.

The cover photograph has been kindly supplied by Getty
Images/Image Bank.